Tom Rogers

SAINT LOUIS

CONTENTS

Series Editors: Thomas J. Doyle and Rodney L. Rathmann

Write to the Library for the Blind, 1333 S. Kirkwood Road, St. Louis, MO 63122-7295 to obtain this study in braille or large print for the visually impaired.

Scripture quotations are taken from the HOLY BIBLE: NEW INTERNATIONAL VERSION®. NIV®. Copyright © 1973, 1978, 1984 by the International Bible Society. Used by permission of Zondervan Publishing House. All rights reserved.

The "NIV" and "New International Version" are registered in the United States Patent and Trademark Office by the International Bible Society. Use of either trademark requires the permission of the International Bible Society.

Copyright © 1997 Concordia Publishing House
3558 South Jefferson Avenue, St. Louis, MO 63118-3968
Manufactured in the United States of America

Introduction

The Godly Man Series

In his letter to the recently established Christian church at Philippi, the apostle Paul likened the Christian life to a race. Paul wrote, "Forgetting what is behind and straining toward what is ahead, I press on toward the goal to win the prize for which God has called me heavenward in Christ Jesus" (Philippians 3:13–14).

Each of us who by faith claims Jesus as Lord and Savior has God's permission and His power to forget "what is behind." Over 2,000 years ago, Jesus came to earth, true God, Son of the eternal Father and yet True Man. Conceived by the Holy Spirit and born of the Virgin Mary, Jesus grew as a boy—through childhood and adolescence—to become a mature man. He endured all the temptations and struggles every man has faced and yet committed no sin of thought, word, or action (Hebrews 4:14–15). According to His Father's plan, He suffered and died on the cross as our substitute, taking our sins upon Himself. We can forget our sins because Jesus' love has overcome our past. He has won the victory over our sins and the constraining, handicapping power of the devil. Jesus showed Himself Lord over sin, death, and the devil when He rose from the dead on Easter morning. We who believe in the crucified, risen, and ascended Savior are made new men by the same Holy Spirit who brought us to faith. As God's Spirit gives us new desires and a new set of goals and priorities, He changes us through the Word of God—the Gospel—so that we come to know God's love and the outpouring of His grace in mighty ways and grow in our relationship with our Father in heaven. Long ago, the psalmist wrote by inspiration of the Holy Spirit the following insight into God and His nature, "His pleasure is not in the strength of the horse, nor His delight in the legs of man; the LORD delights in those who fear Him, who put their hope in His unfailing love" (Psalm 147:10–11).

As we run life's race, our heavenly Father invites us to find our strength and encouragement in Him. His joy is not in any physical means by which men may reach a finish line, such as in the power of a horse or the legs of men. Rather, God finds His joy in those sons who put their hope in Him and in the power of His unfailing love.

God's Word reminds us, "[We] are all sons of God through faith in Christ Jesus" (Galatians 3:26) and our God delights in His relationship with His sons just as every good father prides himself in the growth and accomplishments of his children. He invites us to communicate with Him regularly and often as we experience His Word and respond to His love in prayer.

As we press on toward our heavenly prize, God helps us to live our lives for Him. Many of God's faithful people, both men and women, have lived it before us. Theirs is a heritage for us to build upon and to pass on to those who will follow after us—our wives, children, friends, and others whose lives will be touched by the love and power of God evidenced in our lives.

The writer to the Hebrews encourages us to live as men of faith, reminding us about where to keep our focus as we run life's race: "Therefore, since we are surrounded by such a great cloud of witnesses, let us throw off everything that hinders and the sin that so easily entangles, and let us run with perseverance the race marked out for us. Let us fix our eyes on Jesus, the author and perfecter of our faith, who for the joy set before Him endured the cross, scorning its shame, and sat down at the right hand of the throne of God. Consider Him who endured such opposition from sinful men, so that you will not grow weary and lose heart" (Hebrews 12:1–3).

God's blessings as you run the race and claim the prize already won for you!

About the Godly Man Series

The Godly Man series is especially for men. Written in book-study format, each course in the Godly Man series is organized into chapters suitable for either group or individual study. Periodically throughout each chapter, questions have been provided to further stimulate your thinking, assist you in personal application, and spark group discussion.

How to Use Each Course in the Godly Man Series

Each course in the Godly Man series has been prepared especially for small group settings. It may, however, be used as a self-study or in a traditional Sunday morning Bible class. Chapters of each course may be read in advance of group discussion. Or, participants may take turns reading sections of the Bible study during your group study sessions.

Planning for a Small Group Study

1. *Select a leader* for the course or a leader for the day. It will be the leader's responsibility to secure needed materials, to keep the discussion moving, and to help involve all participants.

2. *Emphasize sharing.* Your class will work best if the participants feel comfortable with one another and if all feel their contributions to the class are important and useful. Take the necessary time at the beginning of the course to get to know one another. Since this course deals with relationship issues, you may ask participants to share their names and a little something about a positive relationship they have now or have had in the past. Share what you expect to gain from this course. Develop an atmosphere of openness, trust, and caring among the participants. Agree in advance that private issues shared during your study will remain within the group.

3. *Pray for one another.* Begin and conclude each study session with a prayer. Pray for one another, for your families, your work, and all other aspects of your life. Involve everyone. Consider praying-around-the-circle, with each person offering a specific prayer to God for the person on his left.

As You Plan to Lead the Group

1. Read this guide in its entirety before you lead the first session.

2. Use the Answers and Comments section in the back of the study.

3. Pray each day for those in your group.

4. Depend on the Holy Spirit. Expect His presence; He will guide you and cause you to grow. God will not let His Word return empty (see Isaiah 55:11) as you study it individually or with others in a group.

5. Prepare well, studying each session's material thoroughly. Add your comments in the margins so that you may add your insights to spark conversation and discussion throughout the session.

6. Begin and end the session with prayer.

7. Begin and end on time. Punctuality is a courtesy to everyone and can be a factor to encourage discussion.

8. Find ways to keep the session informal; consider meeting over breakfast at a local restaurant or some other friendly setting where participants can be seated face to face.

9. Keep the class moving. Limit your discussion to questions of interest to the participants. Be selective. You don't need to cover every question. Note that most Bible references are included in the study guide. At times, however, you may want to look up and share additional insights provided by other suggested Bible references.

10. Build one another up through your fellowship and study. Make a conscious effort to support one another in your personal and professional challenges.

Expect and rejoice in God's presence and blessing as He builds your faith and enriches your life through the study of His Word.

Man as Teacher

Ready

Martin Luther begins each of the six chief parts in his Small Catechism with the words "As the head of the family should teach them (it) in a simply way to his household." With these simple words Luther speaks to all men informing them that God has called them to teach and model righteousness to their families.

Luther isn't simply sharing his own feeling about a man's role as teacher. Instead he reflects the Bible's teaching about the God-given role of man as teacher.

In Deuteronomy 4:1, 9 the Lord addresses Israel: "Here now, O Israel, the decrees and laws I am about to teach you. Follow them so that you may live and may go in and take possession of the land that the LORD, the God of your fathers, is giving you. ... Only be careful, and watch yourselves closely so that you do not forget the things your eyes have seen or let them slip from your heart as long as you live. Teach them to your children and to their children after them."

List five men who have served as teachers to you in your life.

What characteristics do these men have in common?

Teaching by Example
Read

The door of the pastor's office thundered under the strong hand that struck it. A gruff voice bellowed, "I need to speak to you preacher and I need to speak to you right now!" The pastor rose from his seat, said a silent prayer for wisdom, and opened the door. A large, agitated man, whom the pastor recognized as a school parent stood in the doorway. The man's 10-year-old son was at his side. The school principal was standing behind them both. The principal looked as though he would rather be some place else. Without being invited in, the man pushed his way into the pastor's office and asked angrily, "What kind of a school are you running here?" The pastor invited all his guests to sit down. Then he asked the man to repeat his question. "I want to know what kind of school you're running here."

"Please tell me what happened," the pastor responded.

The father began his speech: "One of the troublemaking kids in Jimmy's class has teased him all year long. Jimmy tells me he keeps telling the teacher every time the boy bothers him, but the teacher doesn't do anything about it. After hearing about this troublemaker for about a hundred times, I told Jimmy that the next time that kid gave him any grief he should belt him. I even took him to the backyard to show him how to throw a few punches. Yesterday that boy gave Jimmy a hard time again. Jimmy knew what to do, and this time he did it. He flattened that kid's nose against his face. It was about time. That no good kid needed to learn his lesson. Well, this principal of yours has suspended my Jimmy. For what? For defending himself? I ought to do to him what Jimmy did to that stupid kid! I'm here to tell you preacher that if my boy gets suspended for defending himself, I'm pulling him out of this school!"

Now the pastor looked like he wanted to be someplace else.

The pastor began, "Sir, I'm going to listen to and hear every word you say so it really isn't necessary for you to shout. I know you are upset. I know you believe that your boy is being unfairly punished for fighting. But I believe that the first thing we need to do is to remind you about the kind of school this is. We are a Christian school. That means that neither the principal nor I head this place. The person in charge of this church and school is Jesus. He determines our behavior, and to the best of our ability we follow. Jesus has made it clear that people who live for Him don't believe in the legalistic notion that an eye should be given for an eye and a tooth for a tooth. Instead He tells us to turn the other cheek, to pray for our enemies, and, as far as it is possible, to live in peace with each other. Sir, hitting is not an acceptable solution to a problem here. You've said some rather nasty things about our school, and my dear friend the principal, but I choose not to hit you because of it." At this point the man smirked, but his son's eyes were opened wide. "Instead, I've chosen to try to respect you and your concerns. I've also chosen to speak to you as a child of God, a person God has called me to try to help. Now I don't believe that any problem is ever solved though rudeness or violence. Men of good will solve their problems when they sit together, share their problems, and respect each other enough to commit themselves to resolve their differences. I assure you that I will work hard to resolve your problem. Now I ask you, will you work hard to think and pray your way through this problem instead of trying to bully your way through this problem?" Sheepishly, the man responded, "Yes."

This entire conversation took place in front of the wide eyes of Jimmy.

REACT

1. How would you evaluate the response of Jimmy's dad to his son's suspension? Why?

2. How was Jimmy's dad a teacher in this incident? Was the teaching intentional? What did he teach Jimmy about life?

3. How would you evaluate the pastor's response in this situation?

4. How was the pastor a teacher to Jimmy and his father? What did he teach them? What did he teach them about the kingdom of God?

5. If I found myself in a similar situation I would probably behave like (a) the father or (b) the pastor. Why?

6. How does the pastor's teaching give hope to the world?

The Man Who Teaches Models Love

Read

In the reading from Deuteronomy 4 the Lord addresses the men of Israel and says: "Hear now, O Israel, the decrees and laws I am about to teach you. Follow them so that you may live and may go in and take possession of the land that the LORD, the God of your fathers, is giving you." This passage makes it clear that before a man can teach God's truth, he first has to learn it. In His public ministry Jesus taught His disciples many things. Consider the following passages:

> Jesus replied, " 'Love the Lord your God with all your heart and with all your soul and with all your mind.' This is the first and greatest commandment. And the second is like it, 'Love your neighbor as yourself.' " Matthew 22:37–38

> You have heard that it was said, "Love your neighbor and hate your enemy." But I tell you, Love your enemies and pray for those who persecute you, that you may be sons of your Father in heaven. He causes His sun to rise on the evil and the good, and sends rain on righteous and the unrighteous. Matthew 5:43–45

A new command I give to you: "Love one another. As I have loved you, so you must love one another. By this all men will know that you are My disciples, if you love one another." John 13:34–35

For we are God's workmanship, created in Christ Jesus to do good works, which God prepared in advance for us to do. Ephesians 2:10

REACT

1. What does Jesus teach us in these verses about how we show our love for God?

2. What does Matthew 5:43–45 teach us about dealing with people who continually cause us difficulty? What motivates us to do this? Hint: See Romans 5:6–10.

3. How do we teach others that we are Jesus' disciples?

4. In the passage from Ephesians we learn that in Christ, we are God's workmanship. What is the foundation of these good works? See Ephesians 2:8–9.

Love Is a Verb Not Only a Noun

Read

Jesus wants those who have experienced His love to love all people. The importance of this love is demonstrated in

Jesus' words to Peter and the parable of the unmerciful servant. Read aloud Matthew 18:21–35.

REACT

1. Jesus taught His disciples many things, but forgiveness was central to all of His teaching. Why was forgiveness Jesus' most important teaching?

2. How would the world react to the king who forgave his servant the tremendous debt?

3. How did the king expect the servant to react to his forgiveness?

4. How are we at times like the servant?

5. Why do you suppose the forgiven servant refused to forgive his fellow servant?

6. How might we teach Jesus' forgiveness to our families?

Teaching by Failing
Read

Joe had a very stressful job. There was always more to do than time to do it. But this year was the worst ever. There was more to be done than ever before, and regardless of how hard Joe worked his supervisors were never satisfied. He was constantly being instructed to go faster, work harder, and get more accomplished. He knew his blood pressure was rising and that his anxiety provided him with little opportunity for good sleep. In the middle of his dilemma he remembered how he used to relax himself. In his younger years Joe had smoked. He believed it relaxed him. Joe knew that this was one habit that wouldn't help, only harm, his health. He had been smoke free for over 10 years. But the pressure was so tremendous Joe was tempted to return to the habit. To his surprise and delight the tobacco did seem to relax him. He told himself that he would only use tobacco temporarily. He would only smoke until the pressure at work subsided.

First, Joe would only smoke traveling to and from work and home. As time went on, he found himself becoming all the more addicted to the nicotine. It got to the point where he needed to start smoking at home. Although no one had confronted him directly, Joe's wife and children asked him repeatedly why he smelled like smoke? He always blamed other smokers. Joe's answer didn't sound completely reasonable to his family, but fearing the worst, they chose to believe him until one morning right about daybreak. Joe woke up craving a cigarette and so, wearing his pajamas and robe, went outside to sneak a cigarette. After he had finished the cigarette in his backyard, Joe turned around the corner of his house and ran into his 10-year-old daughter. Joe wondered if she had seen him smoking. His daughter asked why he smelled like smoke. Joe responded that the next door neighbor smokes and that he had run into him just a few moments ago. "The neighbor was smoking," he told his daughter, "and some of the smoke got on me." His daughter didn't say a thing, neither did she change her expression. She just said, "Okay, Dad."

A week later Joe got a phone call from his daughter's principal. Much to everyone's surprise the little girl's teacher had caught her cheating. Joe went to the school. His daughter denied the whole thing, even though the teacher found a "cheat sheet" in her backpack.

Joe assured the principal that he would take care of the problem. As Joe saw it, his daughter had two problems. First, she cheated. Second, she lied about it. Joe began to address the problem as he drove her home from school. Joe turned to his daughter and said, "Tell me why you cheated on the test." She answered with tears streaming down her cheeks, "Dad, the pressure lately has been unbearable. I'm a slow learner, I don't always get everything the teacher wants me to get. And you and Mom want me to get straight A's. I cheated in order to keep from getting into trouble." "All right then," said Joe, "tell me about the lying." "Well Dad, I used to believe that lying was never good but a few weeks ago I caught you smoking in the backyard and you lied about it. Dad, you taught me that sometimes it pays to lie."

Joe had been cut to the core. His daughter had been faced with the same issues he was faced with: expectations that surpassed human reason and an attempt to find something that would reduce her stress. She cheated in order to try and take control of her life and lied in order to stay out of trouble. Joe was very disappointed with his daughter, but most of all with himself.

In his mind Joe concocted potential solutions to this problem.

Surely what his daughter had done was wrong, but Joe had contributed to her problems by teaching her the wrong way to deal with her problems. How could he make the situation right?

React

1. For a moment consider ways in which Joe could make the situation right.

2. What will these possible solutions teach his daughter?

14

Read

Joe decided to confess his sin first to God. In the quiet of his backyard he prayed, "Boy, Lord, I blew it. Not only did I sin against You by relying on nicotine to get me through the pressure on the job, but in trying to hide that sin I lied to my family. Forgive me, Lord, for Jesus' sake." Knowing the promise of God to forgive those who confess their sins, Joe pleaded, "Now, Lord, help me make this right with my family, especially my daughter."

Empowered by God's love for him, Joe confessed his sin to his daughter. She said, "I forgive you, Daddy." Then his daughter turned to Joe and admitted she had cheated at school. Her tears of fear melted to tears of joy as Joe hugged her and spoke quietly, "I forgive you."

React

1. How hard is it for you to confess your sin to a family member. How does knowledge of the forgiveness Jesus won for you on the cross empower and encourage you to seek forgiveness? to give forgiveness?

2. If, by the grace of God, a man can teach his family even through his mistakes, how should we view our own mistakes? the mistakes of others?

The Center of Jesus' Teaching

Read

In his sermon at Antioch of Pisidia recorded in Acts 13, St. Paul informs his hearers of the center of Jesus' message and mission.

"Therefore, my brothers, I want you to know that through Jesus the forgiveness of sins is proclaimed to you. Through Him everyone who believes is justified from everything you could not be justified from by the law of Moses" (Acts 13:38–39).

Paul wants us all to know that the Law of Moses cannot and will not provide sinful people with assurance that we are the children of God. Each time we fail, our response to the Law may be to doubt God's love for us and to wonder whether we are truly saved.

Two pastors of two different denominations met together for lunch. These two men had lots in common since both of their congregations were beginning the construction of new worship facilities. One pastor asked the other how his preaching inspired his people to give the money necessary to build the building. He said simply, "I'm telling them that God loves them, that He sent Jesus to die for their sins, that because of Jesus they are heirs of heaven, and that now they have the opportunity to thank God for His goodness by giving to this program." The pastor who asked the question replied in astonishment, "Is that all you're gonna tell your people? You'll never raise money that way." A little stunned the first pastor asked him how he motivated his people to give. He said, "I tell them that the saved people of God make sure that God receives at least a tithe of everything they make. God loves a cheerful giver."

Such a comment completely ignores all that Jesus did for us on the cross. We are saved by grace, not by works of the Law.

The man of God wants to make sure that he teaches the truth of God's love in Jesus first and foremost to his family. The Gospel frees people: free from guilt and its intimidation, free to love, and free to serve with thankfulness. When the law is preached, people are never free, they are always wondering whether or not they have done enough to earn God's love.

Law and Gospel are not just esoteric theological principles. They are forces we deal with each and every day. They are the identifiers of the way we deal with our world, either as encouragers of people or as discouragers of people.

Because of the death and resurrection of Jesus, all our sins are forgiven and forgotten by God. As men who have experienced the forgiving love of God in Christ Jesus, we desire to share it, to tell it, and to model it to our families so they may experience the magnitude of God's love for them in Jesus.

REACT

1. If you were to ask the average man on the street what he thought Jesus accomplished in His ministry, you might get one of the following responses. Which response is biblical?

a. "He came to show us a new way to live that makes us better people."

b. "He came to give us wisdom that makes our lives easier."

c. "He came to demand a lifestyle that, if kept, will lead to eternal life."

d. "He came to win through His suffering and death the forgiveness of sins for all people. He wants us to know that we will go to heaven not because of what we have done but because of what He has done for us."

2. How might a man teach the forgiveness of sins to his family and friends?

3. What happens in places where the forgiveness of sins is not just believed but practiced?

RESPOND

1. If someone were to ask you where you thought you got the right to teach values, beliefs, and behaviors to your family, what would you say?

2. Teachers are annually reviewed by their principals.

Take a piece of paper, and on the basis of this lesson, write your own self-evaluation as a teacher. Specifically evaluate yourself regarding your attendance in the home, your preparation to teach your family, your effectiveness as a communicator, your success as an example, and your commitment to your students.

3. Teachers regularly prepare lessons plans that tell them what to teach, how to teach it, and to whom it should be taught. Write your own lesson plan as teacher in your family for the next three months.

4. Good teachers are frequently remembered by their students throughout their lives. During class reunions stories are told about teachers who may date back several decades. If today was your last day as a teacher, what stories do you think your students (household) would tell about you? What kinds of stories would you like your students to tell about you, and, what do you need to do in order to make that possible?

MAN AS SpirituAL LEAdER 2

LEAdERs ANd THEiR LEAdERSHip StylE

REAdy

Ask any man on the street to identify men who were great leaders and the list will probably include Ronald Reagan, Vince Lombardi, and Winston Churchill. These men each had a strong, charismatic personality. So strong was their personality that the groups they led were identified not by their achievements but by the strength of their leader.

Jesus was a leader. When Jesus began to gather around Himself people He would lead, He did a strange thing. He didn't surround Himself with the brightest or best the world had to offer. Instead He chose to lead people with obvious shortcomings. Matthew was a tax collector, a much maligned individual. James and John came from a family that sought power and fame. Peter led his life according to the mistaken principle "Fire, ready, aim." Jesus loved them, cared for them, instructed them, and gave them an example to follow when He would leave them. When Jesus left His followers behind they grew strong, they became greater than anyone, including themselves, could have ever imagined. Certainly the biggest reason for that turn around was God who sent forth the Holy Spirit on the day of Pentecost. In addition to the Holy Spirit, Jesus had left them an example, an example of life and an example of leadership. Undoubtedly, after Jesus had ascended into heaven, His disciples had numerous occasions to remember the things that Jesus had said and done. Empowered by the Spirit His disciples witnessed His message of love and forgiveness throughout the world.

Stories of Leadership

Read/React

Summarize the example of leadership Jesus gave to His disciples in each of the following accounts.

Matthew 3:13–17 (especially v. 15)

Matthew 6:1–18

Matthew 7:1–5

Matthew 9:10–13

Respond

Each of us has a fairly clear idea about the kind of leader our family needs. When children are strong willed and difficult, we generally believe they need a strong hand to direct them. When family members show a tendency toward overspending, we generally believe they need a thrifty "penny counter" in order to keep them in line. Put all your preconceived notions behind and place yourself in Jesus' shoes. In His shoes write a description of the kind of leader Jesus would place in your family. After it is written, compare it to your present posture of leadership.

Spiritual Gifts and Spiritual Leaders

Read

Jesus' disciples remembered His leadership. Coupled with the gifts they received from the Holy Spirit, Jesus' disciples grew in their faith and as leaders. As Christian men we desire to see those we lead grow in their faith and leadership ability. The Holy Spirit empowered the disciples to grow and gave them gifts to enable them to lead. The gifts of the Holy Spirit enable us to be spiritual leaders in our homes, churches, and communities.

Scripture informs us that each person who is baptized into Christ is given certain spiritual gifts by the Holy Spirit.

In Romans 12:3–6 Paul acknowledges that we each have different gifts and that God wants us to use these gifts for the good of the whole church.

> For by the grace given me I say to every one of you: Do not think of yourself more highly than you ought, but rather think of yourself with sober judgment, in accordance with the measure of faith God has given you. Just as each of us has one body with many members, and these members do not all have the same function, so in Christ we who are many form one body, and each member belongs to all the others. We have different gifts according to the grace given us.

A careful reading of the New Testament teaches us that the following qualities and abilities are gifts of the Holy Spirit:

From 1 Corinthians 12

Wisdom	Miracles	Prophecy	Discernment
Knowledge	Tongues	Interpretation	Apostleship
Faith	Teaching	Helping	Administration
Healing			

From Romans 12

Prophecy	Service	Teaching	Encouraging
Giving	Leadership	Mercy	

From Ephesians 4

Apostleship	Prophecy	Evangelism	Pastors
Teachers			

From 1 Peter 4

Hospitality	Service	Speaking (prophecy)

Pair off with a member of your group. Once you have decided who your partner will be, go through the list of gifts. Put a check mark next to all the gifts you believe the Holy Spirit has given you. Then go through the list again and this time put a check mark next to all the gifts that you believe your partner has. Then compare your check marks. Do you agree with each other's findings? Are there similarities? Using these gifts, you can provide leadership to your church and to your family. Briefly stated these gifts represent the following characteristics:

Wisdom: The ability to understand the will of God so that you see how events in life and in the church will all work together for good.

Knowledge: The familiarity with the Word of God. Knowing God's attitude and will regarding issues that face individuals and the church.

Faith: The unique ability to believe and so live as though God can and will do great things in the world. This gift is different from the gift of saving faith in Jesus.

Healing: Persons with this gift demonstrate a desire to pray for and minister to the health and healing of others.

Miracles: An extraordinary gift that enables a person to be associated with wonders and signs performed by God.

Prophecy: The ability to speak God's word to people in such a way as to have it understood.

Discernment: The ability to assess which things are helpful for the people of God and which things are not.

Tongues: An extraordinary gift that enables one to speak in languages not known to others.

Interpretation of tongues: The ability to understand and explain a message given to one who speaks in unknown languages.

Apostleship: The ability to speak God's Word in all its truth and to disciple others.

Teaching: The ability to convey God's Word and will effectively.

Helping: The desire to provide assistance to people who have special needs. This may be as simple as setting up tables at church or attending to the gardening needs of the church's exterior.

Administration: The ability to make sure that all things done in a person's life or in the church are done in good order, getting the most out of the gifts we've been given.

Service: This gift is related to helping. It works itself out in a desire to do things for other people in a very quiet, humble way.

Encouraging: The ability to build other people up so that they see themselves as gifted by God and important in the work of the church.

Giving: The desire to give generously of one's treasure for the sake of the Lord. These gifts are given quietly without celebration or attention.

Leadership: The ability to organize and inspire others to accomplish certain tasks in order to build the kingdom of God.

Mercy: This gift enables a heart that is filled with compassion towards the lowly, the meek, the sick, and the poor.

Evangelism: The desire to tell the world about Jesus and the ability to do it easily and effectively.

Hospitality: The ability to open one's heart and home to others. This person makes people feel very welcome and comfortable in their presence.

REACT

A leader is only as strong as the example he sets for others. Identify some spiritual gifts God has provided you. Then answer the following questions:

1. What did I do to deserve this gift?

2. How well have I used this gift to build Christ's church?

3. Put a plan in place that will enable you to use your gifts as a leader in service to Christ's church.

Leading God's Gifted

Read

A pastor once confessed that although he had heard hundreds of sermons throughout his life, he couldn't remember one. The same pastor continued, "But I can easily name five preachers whose lives placed the hand of God upon me." The evangelist John proclaimed, "The Word became flesh and made His dwelling among us. ... full of grace and truth" (1:14) Jesus still comes among His people in Word and Sacrament. As Christ's love works in us, He uses us to come among His people as we share His love and forgiveness won on the cross. Christian men today have the opportunity to place the hand of God upon everyone with whom they come into contact. Whenever we display the faith, love, and forgiveness that Christ gives to us, we place God's hand upon someone else. One of the most powerful ways we can place the hand of God on others is to see them as precious gifts of God full of power and potential. By pointing out the power and potential of others we can lead them to accomplish great things.

A Chinese proverb regarding leadership goes like this: "One of the greatest compliments that can be paid to a leader is to have those whom he has led to the completion of a goal declare: Look what we have done all by ourselves." For the Christian leader, the highest compliment that can be paid is to have those whom he has led say, "Look what the Lord has accomplished through us."

The apostle Paul knew how to lead people in such a way as to see that God alone receives the glory. He begins by reminding them who they are in Christ. Then he declares his thanks to them for what they have accomplished in the kingdom. To the church at Corinth, Paul writes:

> I always thank God for you because of His grace given you in Christ Jesus. For in Him you have been enriched in every way—in all your speaking and in all your knowledge—because our testimony about Christ was confirmed in you. Therefore you do not lack any spiritual gift as you eagerly wait for our Lord Jesus Christ to be revealed. He will keep you strong to the end, so that you will be blameless on the day of our Lord Jesus Christ. 1 Corinthians 1:4–8

The church at Corinth was not a perfect church. It was full of divisions. The church in Corinth allowed immoral behavior to take place in its midst. A man sleeps with his father's wife. Paul is appalled. If that were not enough, they pervert the Lord's Supper. They celebrated it within the context of an agape feast. The affluent members of the church came early to the feast, ate and drank most of the food, and became drunk before the other members arrived.

Paul knew their troubles but instead of relieving his frustration by beating them over the head, he attempts to lead them out of their error by first affirming them. He gives thanks to God for them. This affirmation undoubtedly opens their ears and their hearts to what he has to say.

To the church in Phillipi Paul writes:

> I thank my God every time I remember you. In all my prayers for all of you, I always pray with joy because of your partnership in the gospel from the first day until now, being confident of this, that He who began a good work in you will carry it on to completion until the day of Christ Jesus. ... And this is my prayer: that your love may abound more and more in knowledge and depth of insight, so that you may be able to discern what is best and may be pure and blameless until the day of Christ." Philippians 1:3–6, 9–10

One of the major problems troubling the church at Philippi was legalism. A group of Jewish Christians known as the "Judaizers" invaded churches shortly after Paul left them. They told the Christians that Paul had not told them the whole truth. They insisted that in order to be Christian a person had to first become Jewish. They must be circumcised and observe Jewish dietary laws and worship celebrations. Such teaching bound people's consciences and took away from the sufficiency of Christ. They were leading other people away from the truth that is ours in Christ Jesus.

Despite their error Paul does not judge or condemn them. Instead he uses his spiritual gifts to correct them. Before any correction begins, he lets them know that God had chosen them to accomplish great things in the kingdom. He tells them that he is convinced that God who began a good work in them will bring it to completion in the day of Jesus Christ.

With his words Paul puts his arm around the church at Philippi and encourages them. They know that he prizes them. Paul has proven himself a leader by his love and his example, and so the church listens carefully to his words and follows his direction.

The same wonderful thing can happen when men of God love the people of God and employ their spiritual gifts in service to them.

A pastor was walking through the fellowship hall of the church he served. At the end of the hall he saw that a crowd had gathered around a table. Seeing nothing on the table, the pastor wondered what all the commotion could be about. "What's the matter?" he asked. "It's Dorothy," the people responded. Dorothy was an 8-year-old resident of the home for emotionally disturbed children that was situated right next to the church. The residents of the home came to church and Sunday school every Sunday. Sometimes the rigors of church and Sunday school became too much for them and they would have emotional outbursts. Some of the church members believed that the children disrupted worship and learning and so tried to prevent them from attending.

Knowing all this, the pastor was anxious to resolve this problem with Dorothy. "What's wrong with Dorothy?" the pastor asked. "She won't come out from under the table." "Why did she go under there in the first place?" the pastor asked. "We don't know. But she won't come out." Some people commanded Dorothy to come out from under the table. Others tried to frighten her out by striking and shaking the table. Still others tried to grab her and pull her out. None of these approaches were successful. All they managed to do was to make Dorothy cry. Suddenly the pastor got on his knees and crawled underneath the table. He went over to Dorothy and whispered something in her ear. The pastor then turned around and crawled out from under the table. To everyone's surprise, Dorothy followed.

Everyone wanted to know the magic word the pastor had spoken to Dorothy to get her to come out. The pastor said, "It wasn't a magic word. I just told her that I loved her." Dorothy saw, heard, and felt his love. She was only too happy to follow his lead.

REACT

1. Compare the leadership qualities of Jesus and St. Paul with the qualities of a leader that you admire. In what ways are they the same? In what ways are they different?

2. What is more important about a leader—the things he says, or the way he lives his life?

3. Paul routinely shares his love and respect for Christians who have gone astray. Can you see yourself doing the same thing? What would be the effect of exercising such leadership?

4. Christian leaders frequently appear on television. On the basis of what you have learned in this lesson, what things do effective Christian leaders do in order to lead people to Jesus? What things do they not do?

5. Write the names of three people you lead. Underneath their names make a list of all the spiritual gifts that person demonstrates. Then write the day and the time you intend to affirm that person on the basis of their gifts and thank them for their support.

Spirit-led Leaders Are Honest
Read

A spiritual leader is only as good as his word. Honesty is a godly quality. It shows like a light shining in a dark place. Honest men are a credit to the church, dishonest men discredit the church. Nowhere is this truth more clearly stated than in Acts 4:36–5:5a:

> Joseph, a Levite from Cyprus, whom the apostles called Barnabas (which means Son of Encouragement), sold a field he owned and brought the money and put it at the apostles' feet. Now a man named Ananias, together with his wife Sapphira, also sold a piece of property. With his wife's full knowledge he kept back part of the money for himself, and brought the rest and put it at the apostles' feet. Then Peter said, "Ananias, how is it that Satan has so filled your heart that you have lied to the Holy Spirit and have kept for yourself some of the money you received for the land? Didn't it belong to you before it was sold? And after it was sold, wasn't the money at your disposal? What made you think of doing such a thing? You have not lied to men but to God." When Ananias heard this, he fell down and died.

To the modern-day Christian, Ananias' punishment may seem overly harsh. But Ananias had done more than just withhold money from the apostles. He had mocked the Holy Spirit. Dishonesty is just as common in our time as it was in the days of the early Christian church. God's judgment on those who are dishonest—all sinners—is clear, "The wages of sin is death" (Romans 6:23). Jesus bore that sin for us and rose the victor over it on the third day. God's forgiveness for our dishonesty motivates us to be honest in gratitude for all He has done for us. Honesty is also the product of those who know they have no judgment to fear. Many people lie when they are afraid of the outcome of the truth. God promises to guide us and comfort us in any difficulty we may face.

When Christian men display honesty, taking responsibility for what they have done wrong and trusting God for their deliverance from sin and error, they lift God up as a refuge and strength, an ever-present help in trouble. God is honored by our honesty and the people we lead are blessed by our example.

Spirit-led Leaders Are Humble

Read

James and John the sons of Zebedee, wanted to be exalted in their service to Jesus. Jesus responds to their request for power (Mark 10:35ff) with these words: "You know that those who are regarded as rulers of the Gentiles lord it over them, and their high officials exercise authority over them. Not so with you. Instead, whoever wants to become great among you must be your servant, and whoever wants to be first must be slave of all. For even the Son of Man did not come to be served, but to serve, and to give His life as a ransom for many" (Mark 10:42–45).

Spiritual leaders function with the heart of Christ—putting aside pride. As an example of humility Jesus takes a child, puts him in the middle of the disciples, and declares that unless you receive the kingdom of God like a little child, you shall never enter it. Spiritual leaders are childlike, not childish.

Spiritual leaders realize that the direction in their lives comes not from their own will or ability but from the will of God who loves them and sent His Son to die for them. Spirit-led men give credit for their success to God. They also think of others as being more important than themselves. Therefore they build up their brothers and sisters instead of tearing them down. Men who live humble lives lift Jesus up as Lord, a Lord who is able to change human hearts so that they live for others instead of themselves. People follow men who lead humbly.

Respond

1. For a week, read the newspaper making special note of the leaders headlined in the paper. Make a list of the characteristics these leaders demonstrate. Then evaluate the strengths and weakness of these leaders against the leadership characteristics Jesus empowers us to demonstrate.

2. Conduct family devotions. In so doing you will demonstrate the importance of God's Word to you.

3. Plan to attend church and Sunday school regularly. People are led by a positive role model.

3 MAN AS LOVER

Love Is a Confusing Word

Ready

"Jesus Lover of My Soul" is a favorite hymn of the church. Although its melody is soothing and its words are comforting, one word in the hymn could make the modern man wince—lover. Recently, the word lover has taken on some rather negative connotations. "Lover" describes a person who has accomplished many sexual exploits in his or her life. "Lover" also describes the "significant other" of a person involved in a homosexual relationship.

A word carrying such worldly baggage can be hard to use, especially in something as lovely as a hymn of faith. Jesus provides hope for the word, the hymn, and the world. Jesus was the greatest lover the world has ever known. His ability to function as a lover had nothing to do with His sexual orientation, His good looks, His sophistication, or His income. Jesus was a lover who practiced what He preached. He said, "Greater love has no one than this, that he lay down his life for his friends" (John 15:13).

Jesus defines lover for all time by His selfless death on the cross, a death He faced for those who had rejected Him, mocked Him, and despised Him. Jesus desires that all who believe in Him present themselves to the world as "lovers"— people who are willing to lay down their lives for others.

Love Given, Lost, and Restored

Read

God first demonstrated His love for the world in creation. With great love and power He created a perfect world in six days. As the highlight of the creation He took a pile of clay, formed it into a man, and breathed into this man the breath of life. Even though the wonder and beauty of such great things as the oceans, the mountains, the rivers and streams were at man's disposal to appreciate and enjoy, something was missing from Adam's life. God announced, "It is not good for the man to be alone. I will make a helper suitable for him" (Genesis 2:18).

God caused Adam to fall into a deep sleep. As Adam slept, God removed a rib from his side and used it to fashion a woman. When God brought the woman to Adam, Adam proclaimed, "This is now bone of my bones and flesh of my flesh" (Genesis 2:23). Adam's lonely days were over.

Being perfect, Adam and Eve received each other as a gift from God. The fact that God would bless them with such wonderful companionship only served as further evidence that their God and Creator was a God of love. Adam and Eve's lives focused on God. They served Him as they loved and served each other.

We don't know how long this wonderful existence lasted. We do know that one day their lives changed radically. The devil in the form of a serpent came to Eve and tempted her to eat of the fruit of the tree of the knowledge of good and evil. The devil's argument was persuasive. He seemed to know all of Eve's weaknesses. "The fruit is good for food and a delight to the eyes," the serpent said. Eve agreed but did not eat the fruit. The serpent then gave Eve another reason to eat—one she accepted. He told her the reason God didn't want them to eat of the fruit was "God knows that when you eat of it … you will be like God" (Genesis 3:5). Eve ate the forbidden fruit and shared it with Adam.

Sin entered the world. Adam and Eve quickly learned that their knowledge and wisdom was no match for the challenges that would face them in this now sinful world. When they sinned, the focus of their lives shifted from God to themselves. Adam and Eve now recognized that they were naked. Their nakedness caused them embarrassment and they covered themselves.

When God asked Adam whether or not he had eaten of the forbidden fruit, Adam blames Eve. "The woman You put here with me—she gave me some fruit from the tree, and I ate it" (Genesis 3:12). God asked Eve if she had eaten the forbidden fruit. She blames the serpent.

In response God shows them what it means to be a lover. Instead of immediately ending their lives He chooses to judge them and inform them of the consequences of their behavior. Both their lives will be filled with futility until the day they die. But God promises to do something about the death they have ushered into His world. He will see to it that the seed of the woman will one day crush the head of the seed of the serpent who bruised His heel (Genesis 3:15). This is a clear reference to the birth of Jesus, His death, and His resurrection which would destroy the death that Adam and Eve brought into the world. Moments after they had destroyed His world, God shows His love to Adam and Eve by announcing that Jesus would come to lay down His life for all sinners.

When Jesus became flesh and dwelt among us, He did not seek to be served but instead came to serve and to lay down His life for many. Jesus was a "lover." He gave and He gave and He gave, even to the point of giving His life. Today Jesus calls each of His disciples to love in the same selfless way that He has loved them in all their relationships, but especially in their marriages.

REACT

1. Your wife may not be the same as when you first married. She may now have gray hair, a larger waistline, or a more cautious spirit. Her ability to please you without even trying may have given way to an ability to disappoint or frustrate you. How can your attitude affect your relationship to your wife? How does Jesus, the lover of your soul, enable you to continue to love as He has loved?

2. The men in your office enjoy talking about the women in your office. Much of what is said about the women is sexual in nature. When you question your co-workers about this kind of talk, they become upset with you and tell you that this kind of behavior is normal and harmless. In light of Jesus' love, how would you describe this behavior?

3. Think of a time when someone treated you more like a thing than a person. How did that make you feel? What, if anything, do you think you could have done to make them treat you as a person?

4. Work places throughout the nation have posted notices that inform people what to do in the event that they are sexually harassed. What would happen to incidents of sexual harassment as people recognized others as sinners for whom Jesus suffered and died?

Laying Down Your Life for Your Friends

Read

Jesus would have us be lovers to all—to treat everyone as a person for whom we would lay down our lives. With that in mind read and react to the following situation:

Deborah and Donald were both raised in Christian households. Deborah's high school years seemed to be "perfect." She became a National Merit Scholar. She was also extremely attractive. Her good looks coupled with her athletic ability enabled her to become a cheerleader and an outstanding volleyball player. She was homecoming queen her senior year. Throughout her years in high school she always had a boyfriend. Deborah was never home alone on a Saturday night.

Donald was also gifted with great academic ability. He was the valedictorian of his high school class. He enjoyed success as an athlete, was elected student body president in his senior year, and also was considered a "hunk" by most of the young women in his high school.

Deborah and Donald met in college at a fraternity "rush" party. They were immediately attracted to each other. They began to date. Dating Donald brought Deborah much attention. Her girl friends continually reminded her how fortunate she was to have such a good-looking, gifted, young man as Donald. After they had dated for two months, Deborah's girl friends began to inquire as to whether or not she and Donald had sex.

Donald's experience was similar. With Deborah on his arm at school and fraternity events, he became greatly envied. Soon after he and Deborah became an "item," his friends and fraternity brothers began to encourage him to become sexually intimate with Deborah. Some of his friends even began to tease him when he shared that he had yet to "be" with Deborah.

Both Donald and Deborah enjoyed the attention they received. It fed their already well-developed egos. When winter came, Donald's fraternity brothers made plans to enjoy a ski weekend together. Couples who went on this ski weekend occupied the same room. Knowing full well what it meant to take a "date" to the ski weekend, Donald asked Deborah to go with him. Deborah knew that this was not just an opportunity to ski. She knew she would be expected to become sexually active with Donald. This knowledge not only excited her but also alarmed her.

REACT

1. What would you say to Donald about this trip if you were his father? his pastor? Would there be any difference between what you would say and what the pastor would say?

2. What would you say to Deborah about this trip if you were her father? her pastor? Would there be any difference between what you would say and what the pastor would say?

3. As Donald's dad you have learned that Donald took Deborah on the ski weekend and had sexual intercourse. What would you say to him? How does what you say reflect what you believe?

4. You as Deborah's father learn that Deborah went on the ski weekend and had sexual intercourse with Donald. What would you say to her? How does what you say reflect what you believe?

5. Given the fact that Jesus teaches that love is not measured by sexual activity but by one's ability to serve others, how would He counsel Deborah and Donald?

Love and Marriage

Read

Ephesians 5 gives direction for family relationships. "Wives, submit to your husbands as to the Lord. For the husband is the head of the wife as Christ is the head of the church, His body, of which He is the Savior" (Ephesians 5:22–23). These words taken out of context have given some husbands "permission" to expect or to force their wives to submit to them. If the wife should ever refuse to submit, her husband might tell her she has violated the will of God.

Although men often quote Ephesians 5:22 to describe the way wives should relate to their husbands, Ephesians 5:21 and 23 are often ignored. Ephesians 5:21 reads: "Submit to one another out of reverence for Christ." These words serve as the "topic sentence" for what is to follow. Having made it clear that Jesus wants husbands, wives, and children to submit to one another, Paul moves forward and explains how each group submits to the other. Wives submit to their husbands who act first to serve their wives. Husbands submit to wives who love them like Christ loved the church and laid down His life for her. Children submit to their parents who have loved them.

React

1. Describe how men who cite Ephesians 5:22 out of context might treat their wives.

2. How do Ephesians 5:21 and 23 place into proper context the concept of "submission" spoken of in verse 22?

3. How might a husband respond as he is empowered by Jesus to lay down his life for his wife?

Laying Down Your Life

Read/React

Circle the answer which you believe most accurately reflects the will of Jesus, the "lover" in each situation. Be prepared to explain the reason for your answer.

1. Your 17-year-old son has begun to dress in a manner that shocks you. You are also surprised by the amount of time he spends worrying about his hair, his clothes, and the kind of car he wants to own. You ask him why his appearance is suddenly so important to him. He responds, "So I can get girls." How would you respond as you are motivated by Jesus, the lover of your soul?

a. I completely understand young man. I'm happy to see that you're growing up to be a healthy male.

b. Sow your wild oats while you can, son, the day is coming when you will be completely tied down.

c. Instead of worrying about "getting girls," try being the best friend possible to the girls in your school. This will help you to build relationships with them.

2. A single woman living on your street is a frequent topic of conversations among your married male neighbors. One of your neighbors states that he hears that this woman is looking for a physical relationship but doesn't want to make a long-term commitment. How might you respond as you are motivated by Jesus, the lover of your soul?

a. She needs to look no further, I am the right man for her.

b. She needs a lover who loves as Jesus has loved me.

c. I envy the guy who gets to sleep with her.

d. Why would someone want to marry if they don't have too? Maybe some lucky guy could just live with her.

e. I'll pray that she finds a man who will commit himself to her and her to him.

3. Your best friend is 40 years old and single. One day on the golf course he shares with you the fact that he is a virgin. How would you respond as you are motivated by Jesus, the lover of your soul?

a. Ha. Ha. Ha. Ha. Ha.

b. What is your sexual orientation?

c. You've got to be kidding. No healthy 40-year-old, red-blooded, American man is a virgin.

d. I'm really proud of you but not as proud as the woman whom God has chosen to be your wife.

4. Your wife has asked you to be more expressive with your feelings. She explains how good it makes her feel when you hold hands in public and she wishes you would spend more time just holding her. How might the man of God respond to such a request?

a. I think holding hands in public is for kids and wimps. I don't care what you need, I'm not doing it if it makes me feel uncomfortable.

b. I would think you'd outgrow such foolishness.

c. I'll start giving you more of what you want if you start giving me more of what I want.

d. I hear what you're asking, and I will do the best I can.

5. You have discovered that your 17-year-old son is sexually active. You tell him that such behavior is not healthy for him at this time of his life. How might you respond?

a. She could become pregnant and your life would be over from that point.

b. You might catch AIDS or another STD.

c. Abortions are awfully expensive.

d. God has reserved the sacredness of sex for people who are married. By having sex with this girl now, you both take from each other something you have no right to take.

Respond

1. Make a list of things you can do for your wife that will enable her to see that you are ready to lay down your life for her.

2. Make a list of things you can do for your children that will enable them to see that you are ready to lay down your life for them.

3. Jesus, the lover of your soul, empowers you to be a lover. How can you demonstrate in words and by actions that the lover of your soul has recreated you to love?

4. List times when you have loved yourself more than friends and so have acted in a less than God-pleasing matter. Confess those sins to Jesus the lover of your soul and in faith experience the joy of His love and forgiveness.

MAN AS FATHER

Abba! Father!

Ready

Galatians 4:4–7 reads: "But when the time had fully come, God sent His Son, born of a woman, born under law, to redeem those under the law, that we might receive the full rights of sons. Because you are sons, God sent the Spirit of His Son into our hearts, the Spirit who calls out, 'Abba! Father!' So you are no longer a slave, but a son; and since you are a son, God has made you also an heir."

In this passage we see the essence of fatherhood. History has recorded the names and characteristics of many fathers. Abraham, Isaac, and Jacob are the "fathers" of Israel. George Washington is the father of our country. Hippocrates is known as the father of modern medicine. All these men have one thing in common—greatness. But greatness can never be assumed, it always has to be earned. How do fathers today earn that greatness?

A recent Father's Day card perhaps provides the definition of greatness in fatherhood today: "Almost anyone can be a father, but it takes someone special to be a Dad."

God has created the world in such a way as to ensure that most men can become fathers. It is a purely biological phenomenon. No man ever had to study material on fatherhood and pass a test before his voice changed and he became biologically capable of becoming a father. It's not that easy to become a dad.

In order to call a father "dad" a relationship of love must exist between the child and his/her father. If the father does not enter a close, loving relationship with his child, then the child will never be able to apply the title "dad" to the man responsible for his/her life. Scripture seems to lift up the "office of dad."

On what must have been the most difficult night in His life, the night in which He was betrayed, Jesus sought support. He looked for support from his inner circle of disciples, Peter, James, and John. They slept as Jesus anticipated His time of need and sorrow. As Jesus opened His heavy heart to His Father, He used the familiar "Abba" to address Him (Mark 14:36). "Abba Father" is equivalent to "daddy." Imagine the power of that moment. The one who opened the eyes of the blind, healed the lame, turned water into wine, fed 5,000 with a few loaves of bread and fish, and stilled storms, needed the help of His Father in order to face His final objective. Jesus' prayer is not filled with sophisticated speech that one might use to address a national leader. Instead He calls His Father Daddy and asks for help. So confident is He in the love of His Daddy that He asks Him to take this cup—sorrow and suffering—from Him. Without apology He stands in the strength of His Daddy's love and understanding and says: "Abba, Father, all things are possible to You; remove this cup from Me; yet not what I will, but as You will." Jesus did fulfill His Daddy's will as He suffered and died on the cross for the sins of the whole world. The resurrection of Jesus from the dead demonstrates to the world the approval of Jesus' "Daddy." Jesus had accomplished the purpose for which He came to earth—to win victory for us over sin, death, and the power of Satan.

Through Jesus' death we have access to God as Father—Daddy. He brings His sons and daughters into the world with reason and purpose. He provides for their needs. He protects them from evil. He listens to their every prayer. He forgives all their sins, and He has prepared for them a mansion in heaven. Our Daddy in heaven empowers us as His sons to love and provide for our children with the same kind of love He has for us.

Biblical Characteristics of Dads

Read

Good dads understand timing. At the fullness of time God sent forth His Son, and He sent signs that indicated it was time for the Messiah to come. The angel visits the Virgin Mary. She becomes pregnant with the Savior of the world. Joseph receives a visit from an angel letting him know that it was time for him to put aside the Jewish rules of decency and to take this unmarried pregnant woman into his house. The Wise Men knew that the time had come for the Messiah to be born when God set His star in the east.

A man who longs to become a dad in the very image of His heavenly Father will wait for that day to happen. A baptized man of God will make sure he does not place himself in a position where he can become a father until God provides His signs that he is ready. Those signs include a mature lifestyle, an ability to provide for a family, and a wedding ring. Baptized men of God resist the temptation to have sexual activity outside of marriage. Marriage is a sign to the man and to the world that this woman is the spouse of God's choosing and that the man and woman have a relationship especially conducive for raising children.

Other facets of fatherhood require a sense of timing as well. A man who becomes a dad knows that it is not always time to say yes to his children, nor is it always time to say no to his children. Again, the signs are there. If a 16-year-old child who has repeatedly been in trouble around home, church, and school asks for a driver's license, a good dad knows that it is not the proper time to lay this 2,000 pound responsibility into his child's lap. In the same way a good dad knows that if a 16-year-old who has demonstrated responsibility requests a driver's license, it is time, time to say yes.

A good dad also knows that whether it is time to say yes or no, it is always time to explain the decision to the child. Even when the child cannot accept the words of the father because of hurt, anger, or immaturity, a good dad still has the responsibility of speaking to his child the reasons and circumstances that led to the decision. Even when the answer is yes, it is important for the child to know what they have done in order to deserve a yes. Such an explanation gives direction and inspiration to the child so that they can continue to accomplish great things.

A good dad knows the time to bless his child as she/he moves from stage to stage in life. When a father sees his young child growing in confidence and in ability to be kind and respectful, he knows it is time to bless his child's request to spend the night at someone else's home. When the child grows further in responsibility and wisdom, the father knows it's time to let her/him go with a friend to a movie. When the child grows still further in responsibility and wisdom, a good dad knows when it's time to allow the child to date, go off to college, and finally get married. A good dad who has involved himself in the life of the child will see that the child seeks the blessing of the father as they move through the various stages in life. Blessed is that dad.

A good dad also knows when it's time for him to take certain steps and actions in his role as a father. He knows when it is time to go and find out what is happening in the life of a child who has spent the entire evening alone in her/his bedroom. He knows when it is time to present himself to the child's teacher to see what can be done at home in order to help the child make academic progress. A good dad knows that there is never a time when the child should not be growing in grace and so he sees to it that he brings his family to the services of God's house and provides for their further instruction in the faith. A dad who sees his child as a gift of God knows he has a responsibility to set a good example for his children in regards to spiritual life. He attends church. He attends Bible class. He participates in his congregation's ministry. He knows that there is never a time when he will not have enough time to lead his children to Jesus.

A good dad knows when an action he has taken is God-pleasing and right and sticks to it, even when it does not receive the thanks of his family. A good dad also knows when an action he has taken is not God-pleasing and right. He knows that at these times he needs to ask for the forgiveness of his family. A good dad who knows when it is time to confess his wrong is a tremendous blessing and model for his children. A father who can ask for forgiveness lets his children know the importance of their respect for him.

REACT

1. What do you think about the notion that God sends us "signs" that let us know when certain behaviors and privileges are appropriate or inappropriate for our children?

2. When a dad sees that it is time to allow his children to take certain steps in life, how can the father be confident in his decisions? What role does faith play in a father's ability to help his children grow through the various stages of life?

3. Dads who are busy supporting their family may have precious little extra time. Do church and Bible class, family devotions, and being involved in the ministry of the congregation come under the heading "if time permits"? How might this attitude be dangerous?

4. A wise father once told his teenage son who seemed to have an opinion about everything that God had created him with two ears and one mouth. This fact suggested a ratio of use. Does this "rule" also apply to dads? If so, how?

5. Many fathers believe that it is important for them to be right all the time. In order to keep this image alive in the minds of their children, they often defend their actions and decisions as though they were sacred truth. How does a father's confession of sins affect relationships in the home?

Dad the Merciful

Read

Praise be to the God and Father of our Lord Jesus Christ, who has blessed us in the heavenly realms with every spiritual blessing in Christ. For He chose us in Him before the creation of the world to be holy and blameless in His sight. In love He predestined us to be adopted as His sons through Jesus Christ, in accordance with His pleasure and will. Ephesians 1:3–5

Our Father in heaven redeemed us. His Son, Jesus, paid the price to buy us back from sin, death, and the power of the devil through His death on the cross. In fact, above all the attributes of God revealed in the Scripture, His mercy is mentioned the most. If we gave our children the opportunity to identify the characteristic their father displays most often, what would it be?

Our Abba Father provides us a sterling example of Dad as merciful Redeemer. When the earth became so filled with sin and rebellion that God exclaimed that He was sorry He ever created people, He sent a great flood to destroy every living creature. He had decided to destroy the world, but not until He had chosen a man and his family to save. He made sure that He had demonstrated mercy by taking steps necessary to redeem humanity before the first drop of rain started. After the flood, those He had promised to redeem did not remain faithful to Him either. They lived their lives selfishly, doing great injustices to one another, and worshiping and honoring other gods. But their Father in heaven did not wipe them off the face of the earth. Instead, He sent them judges and prophets, men and women, who would speak faithfully His life-changing word of truth to them. Some responded, some did not. God did not give up. Instead He kept sending prophets as His agents who would reveal the truth—His desire for them to be His people.

When the nation of Israel found itself in bondage in Egypt, God did not ignore their pleas for help, even though most of them didn't even know His name (Exodus 3:13–14). Instead, He raised up Moses as their leader, showed His strength to the Egyptians through the plagues, and finally sent the angel of death to destroy every firstborn in Egypt and to drive Pharaoh into releasing the people of Israel from their bondage. When they set out into the hot sun and deep darkness of the wilderness, He sent pillars of cloud and fire to guide them. When Egypt pursued them in order to once again take them captive, God rescued them by opening up the Red

Sea so they could pass in safety. He then caused the waters of the sea to go back to their previous position thus destroying Pharaoh and his army. Later in their lives, He rescued them from their exile in Assyria and Babylon, an exile they deserved because of their disobedience.

And then ... in the fullness of time He demonstrated His mercy by sending His only begotten Son into the world to redeem the world by His death.

The Scripture makes it clear, God does not desire to punish His children. Instead God reveals His mercy and love to all people through His Law—that shows them their sin and desperate need for a Savior—and His Gospel—the forgiveness of sins and eternal life He won for all people through His Son's death on the cross. In the same way, we as earthly fathers proclaim both Law and Gospel to our children—to reveal to them our mercy and our love.

Earthly fathers tell stories of personal strength that enabled them to let their children experience the consequences of their behavior: walking to school because they refused to get up and missed the bus or letting a child stay in jail for something he has done. Some fathers are filled with pride as they recount how they "threw their child out of the house" because of their disobedience. Certainly punishment for disobedience is appropriate, but the punishment must never be an end in itself. Punishment must ultimately serve the purpose of once again demonstrating mercy to the child. A father who allows his son to remain in jail must make sure that he is the very first visitor the son receives the next day. This will go a long way toward teaching the child that imprisonment is not a way for his father to "get even with him" but instead the father's attempt to once again demonstrate love and mercy.

Luke 15:11–32 tells the well-known story of the prodigal son. Perhaps this story has been misnamed. It may just as well be the parable of the father who was a dad. This unnamed father could have easily refused to let his selfish son come home. He could have also just as easily refused to give his son the inheritance that got him into trouble in the first place. Instead he was gracious to his son. He gave him the inheritance and when he had squandered it, welcomed him back into the safety of his home. The father's love demonstrated mercy. Certainly some—especially the older brother—considered the father's love and mercy foolish and unfair. That will always be the case. The world is offended by love, mercy, and grace. Christian dads pray that God will enable them to conform their actions to His heart, demonstrating endless mercy and love.

React

On the basis of mercy consider the following common phrases spoken by parents:

1. A parent's job is simple, just teach the kid right from wrong.

2. At least I put that kid in his place.

3. He got himself into trouble, he can get himself out. I'm not doing anything to help.

4. That's my kid's problem not mine. Let him deal with it.

5. If you keep bailing those kids out, they will never grow up.

Adoption

Read

God sent His Son, born of a woman, born under law, to redeem those under law, that we might receive the full rights of sons. Galatians 4:4–5

God became a Father when He created Adam and Eve. But Adam and Eve rebelled against God, sinned, and so divorced themselves from the Father. Adam and Eve were ungrateful children. They rejected their loving Father when they ate from the tree. They even lied to their Father when He questioned them about their actions. Adam and Eve separated themselves from God.

We could all understand an earthly father who after being divorced by his children would say he would never want to enter into that kind of relationship again. It cost him way too much. God's ways are not our ways, neither are His thoughts our thoughts. So we stand in awe of a God who would want to adopt the very children who had rejected Him.

When St. Paul uses the word *adoption* he refers to the Roman system of adoption, a complicated process. It began with the natural father. The natural father of a child possessed great power and authority. In fact a young man within the Roman empire couldn't be emancipated until the death of his father. This made adoption very difficult because the child would have to pass out of the authority of one father into the power and authority of another. That's precisely why St. Paul tells us that "God sent His Son, born of a woman, born under law, to redeem those under law." God in Christ overcame the authority of the one who took possession of us in our sin— Satan. God didn't just carefully convince the devil to give up authority over us, He defeated him through His Son's death on the cross. He took authority back so He could adopt us.

A Roman father whose son was to be adopted by another man would begin a process known as "mancipatio" (from which our English word *emancipation* comes). In this process the natural father would sell his son to the adopting father three times. The first two times he would buy him back, but the third time he would not. The devil daily would buy us back from God. Our free will was his method of payment. Our fallen will is no match for the devil's temptations. But rather than allow us to remain in the deadly clutches of the devil, God raised the price He would pay for the privilege of adopting us. No longer offering just our will and desire to be with Him, He offered the death of His own sinless Son. Satan could not match such an offering. The offering of God's own Son paralleled the Roman father's third attempt to sell his son. This time he didn't buy him back. In our case, through the death of Jesus, the devil couldn't buy us back. We belonged to God. In the Roman system the announcement that the adopting father had paid the price for his new child was known as the "vindicatio." Indeed the death and resurrection of Jesus is the vindication for all who believe in Him.

Adoption in Rome meant that the family who gave up the son lost all rights to him. The devil has lost all claim to us. The adopted child gained all the legal rights of his new family, he also became heir to his new father's estate. The adopted child's old life was completely wiped out. All his old debts were canceled. He was truly a new man with a new life.

In Christ we have said good-bye to our life and have received the new "rights" of a child of God. We are truly new people, the old has gone away, behold the new has come. All our old debts have been paid in full by Jesus, the Son of our adopting Father.

Earthly dads who possess saving faith in Jesus desire to be this kind of Father. First, we want to be men in whose life the love of God is powerfully present. That love will enable us always to love our children even when they reject us. We pray that God would empower us to do whatever it takes to love our children with the kind of love revealed by our heavenly Father when He sent His only Son to die for us. We will strive to show them Jesus every day in every way. We too will welcome our children into our lives daily as new creatures.

REACT

Unfortunately there have been instances when parents who have adopted children have lived to regret their decision. God has never regretted the fact that He adopted us. Our Abba! Father! loves us unconditionally.

1. St. Paul knew that all children adopted by God through the blood of Christ were new creatures. God would never hold their past against them. What does this say to us as we greet our children each morning? What does the principle of the new life say to us when we fail in our role as "dads"?

2. A man who was adopted as an infant was frequently asked how he felt about being adopted. His response was clear and powerful. "I feel wonderful. Children are most often born to parents who have a legal obligation to love them. I was adopted by parents who had a gospel obligation to love me." In short he always knew that he was wanted. How can we make sure our children always feel wanted?

Call Me Daddy, Please!

Read

A young woman became deathly ill with cancer. After several futile attempts to eradicate the disease by other means, her physician informed her that her only hope was a bone marrow transplant. Family members and friends were tested immediately. No suitable match was found. The physician asked the woman if there were any other relatives. She hesitated. Finally her fear of death caused her to overcome her reservation and she mentioned her father, a father she had stopped speaking to 15 years earlier. The physician urged her to contact her father. Reluctantly, she did.

The separation between the woman and her father was the result of a lifetime of conflict. As far as she was concerned, her father was way too demanding. As far as the father was concerned, she was way too irresponsible. She prayed they could put the past behind them and start anew.

God's love enabled the daughter and father to put the past behind them. The father proved to be a suitable match. A day for the procedure was set. After the father had painfully given his bone marrow and the procedure for placing it into his daughter had begun, the father was wheeled into the recovery room. His pastor was waiting for him there. After a few moments of small talk the pastor told the father that he had prayed that the transplant would "take." The father's eyes immediately filled with tears. He opened his quivering lips and said, "Pastor, I hope so too, but I believe I have already received my miracle." "How so?" the pastor asked. The father shared with the pastor that while they were waiting for surgery, he had turned to his daughter and said, "Honey, I love you." And she responded, "I love you too, daddy." "After all the years and all the anger, Pastor, we're finally a family again."

Jesus also knew that His life depended upon His Father. He knew that His Father loved Him. He died certain that God would receive the sacrifice of His life as payment for the world's sin. Jesus was confident in His Father's goodness and love.

React

1. What does use of the word *daddy* communicate?

2. Try to make a list of the things that Jesus believed about His Father that enabled Him to call Him "Daddy." Then, make a list of the things that present-day children must believe about their father in order to call him "daddy." Compare the two lists. Which of these qualities do you possess?

Dads Leave an Inheritance for Their Children

Read

Galatians 4:7 continues, "You are no longer a slave, but a son; and since you are a son, God has made you also an heir."

Two men waiting to see a physician started up a conversation. They began to speak about how heredity affects a person's life. After sharing a few words about eye color, hair retention, and propensity towards cancer, their conversation turned to what both their deceased parents had left them. The one man had been left a business which he had trouble running. In addition to the business he had received a home, a fortune, and the scorn of many of his friends and family members who declared he did not deserve it. The other man mentioned that his father had left him an example of honesty, integrity, love, and faith.

React

1. Of the two inheritances which one was most valuable? Why?

2. Make a list of the things that you will be able to leave your children, both material and spiritual. Then ask your children to make their own list of the things they believe you will leave them as an inheritance. Conpare the lists.

Respond

1. We began by sharing the message of a Father's Day card, "Almost anyone can be a father, but it takes a special man to be a dad." How do you feel about that statement now?

2. Some men may truly desire to be "dads" for their children but have no positive role model to draw from. According to our lesson, who can serve as a role model for dads? How will this be reflected in words and actions?

3. Sometimes, for a variety of reasons, relationships between father and their children don't turn out the way either one would have liked. What word does our Abba Father have to say to those of us who have regrets regarding our parenting?

5 MAN AS PROVIDER

Leadership Style and Purpose

Ready

In 1997 Evander Holyfield fought the heavyweight champion Mike Tyson. After a long hard fight that went more than 10 rounds, Holyfield defeated Tyson. Reporters flooded the ring looking for an opportunity to interview the new champion. When the reporters finally had his attention they asked him questions about the fight. "What was your fight plan, Evander?" "Was Tyson slower than you thought he would be?" "Was it your plan to box him in the early rounds, tire him out, and then put him away in the later rounds?" Regardless of the question, Holyfield's answer was the same: "I had no plan for this fight, the Holy Spirit fought this fight for me, I give all the glory to God."

Regardless of the sport, many professional athletes give credit to God for their success. Reggie White of the Green Bay Packers gave God credit for his team's victory in the Super Bowl. Bob Wetland of the New York Yankees likewise gave credit to God for his team's victory in the World Series. Gary Gaetti, while playing with the St. Louis Cardinals, likewise credited God for his team clinching the Central Division Title of the National League. When the cameras are on and the world is watching, many Christian athletes set themselves apart from other athletes by declaring their faith in God.

Somehow that posture changes when it comes time to negotiate contracts. When athletes, even Christian athletes negotiate new, lucrative contracts, they generally make the same statement, "I have to do the best I can for myself and my family."

Somehow when the conversation turns to money, there is usually no reference made to one's trust in God. When it comes to money, guidance seems to come from within. Athletes aren't the only men who at times are tempted to believe that they, and they alone, are responsible for their income. Many men affirm "the Lord helps those who help themselves."

The Bible tells a different kind of story. According to Scripture, "The eyes of all look to You, and You give them their food at the proper time. You open Your hand and satisfy the desires of every living thing" (Psalm 145:15–16). "The LORD will guide you always; He will satisfy your needs in a sun-scorched land and will strengthen your frame" (Isaiah 58:11).

In Scripture God clearly states that men do not provide for themselves and their families, He does.

Leading toward Peace

Read

It used to be rare for a woman to experience a heart attack. Heart attacks seemed to be the sole possession of men who worked hard and worried about providing for their families. After World War II, women who had worked outside the home in order to support the war effort remained in the workforce in order to supplement their family incomes. The ensuing decades saw more and more women working outside the home. Home life was changing. As the divorce rate continued to rise, together with the cost of living, women, in many cases, needed to work. As they worked, many women experienced a discrepancy between what men were paid and what women were paid for doing the same job. They demanded equality in pay for equality in responsibility. As salaries increased for women, so did responsibilities and expectations. In a few short decades women seeking to provide for themselves and their families had increased their chances of having a heart attack.

In the 1980s stress was a word on everyone's lips. It seemed unfair that people should have to pay such a high price for trying to provide for themselves.

People felt that way 2,000 years ago. Even then men and women worried themselves sick about preserving their lives. That's why in His first recorded sermon, the Sermon on the Mount, Jesus said:

Look at the birds of the air; they do not sow or reap or store away in barns, and yet your heavenly Father feeds them. Are you not much more valuable than they? Who of you by worrying can add a single hour to his life? And do you worry about clothes? See how the lilies of the field grow. They do not labor or spin. Yet I tell you that not even Solomon in all his splendor was dressed like one of these. If that is how God clothes the grass of the field, which is here today and tomorrow is thrown into the fire, will He not much more clothe you, O you of little faith? So do not worry, saying, "What shall we eat?" or "What shall we drink?" or "What shall we wear?" For the pagans run after all these things, and your heavenly Father knows that you need them. But seek first His kingdom and His righteousness, and all these things will be given you as well. Therefore do not worry about tomorrow, for tomorrow will worry about itself. Each day has enough trouble of its own. Matthew 6:26–34

React

1. How difficult is it for a modern man to trust that God will adequately provide for him and his family? Why?

2. Comment on the phrase "God helps those who help themselves."

3. Jesus instructs us to seek His kingdom first because He provides for all our needs. Almost all of us know how to seek a living, but how can we seek first His kingdom?

Enough Is Enough

Read

A man once told his co-workers that he intended to work at his job until he turned 70 years old. You can imagine the surprise of his co-workers when the man suddenly announced on his 61st birthday that he had decided to retire at 62. At his retirement party friend after friend asked him why he had decided to retire so "early." His response was simple but profound, "I always told myself I wanted to work until I had enough, and one day I asked myself, how much is enough? I decided I had enough and so I am going to devote the rest of my life to serving others."

How much is enough? Common answers to that question include: "Enough to allow me to do what I want to do when I want to do it." "Enough to support me in the lifestyle I am accustomed to." "Enough to leave something for my children." St. Paul responds to "how much is enough?" with these words: "We brought nothing into the world, and we can take nothing out of it. But if we have food and clothing, we will be content with that" (1 Timothy 6:7–8). St Paul says food and clothing are enough. Jesus Himself tells us regarding His own possessions: "Foxes have holes and birds of the air have nests, but the Son of Man has no place to lay His head" (Matthew 8:20).

The Bible's comments on what amount of income or possessions is required to sustain life immediately direct us to the question of the meaning of life. The world would tell us that purpose in life is found in acquiring things, attaining things, and conserving those things you have attained and acquired. You earn all you can and then keep all that you can.

The world would suggest that satisfaction from all this acquiring and conserving comes from being able not just to eat but to eat the things you want to eat. Satisfaction, to the world, comes when one not only has clothes to wear but has designer clothes to wear. Satisfaction comes also from having more possessions than others. The amount of material goods that I have accumulated indicate my success.

1. How successful would man measure his life if all he had provided for his family was food and clothing?

2. How would God measure a man's success in providing for his family?

Is Money the Root of All Evil?

Read

St. Paul tells Timothy: "People who want to get rich fall into temptation and a trap and into many foolish and harmful desires that plunge men into ruin and destruction. For the love of money is the root of all kinds of evil. Some people, eager for money, have wandered from the faith and pierced themselves with many griefs" (1 Timothy 6:9–10). Paul clearly indicates that money itself is not the root of all evil, instead the *love* of money is.

Very often Christian men confuse their desire to provide for their families with their love of money. Money in our culture is more than just the means by which we keep our family happy and healthy. Money can be the determiner of greatness, a source of high self-esteem, and a possession that makes us attractive to others. For fallen men anything that offers greatness, self-esteem, and attractiveness is easily loved and sought after. The love of money gets us into trouble because it involves us in a futile attempt to make ourselves worthy.

Scripture would suggest that greatness, self-esteem, and attractiveness are not functions of possessing money but instead functions of our relationship with God. God provides for people. God declares us "good and faithful servants." The love of God in Christ Jesus and our service in response to that love makes us pleasing to God. The love of God provides us with greatness, self-esteem, and attractiveness. This is why Jesus tells us that we are to seek first the kingdom of God and His righteousness and all these things will be added to us as well.

React

Consider the following:

Can a man be great, full of self-esteem, and someone people want to have in their lives if:

he never owns his own home?

he can't afford to send his children to private schools or even to college?

he has never taken his wife to Hawaii or any other popular vacation spot?

he's never owned a new car?

We Have More to Support than Our Families

Read

Jesus has called all His people to love the Lord their God with all their heart, with all their soul, and with all their mind. One key word in this passage is "all." This passage would suggests that God wants more than a tithe of what He provides, He wants it all.

Churches throughout the land and your own local congregation are faced with tremendous challenges and opportunities for ministry. Mission work in this country and overseas is desperately needed. Christian groups in this country are committed to everything from supporting unwed mothers who choose to have their children, to providing Christian counseling for families and individuals, to offering relief aid to those whose lives have been disrupted by a natural disaster. The church of Jesus Christ has always been able to identify more places and ways to do ministry than it has money.

1. When they think of themselves as providers, most men believe that they need to support themselves and their family. What additional desire does God's Spirit bring to those who through faith belong to God in Christ Jesus?

2. How can we who may have limited wealth support the ministry of our church?

If God Is Our Provider, Where Do We Fit In?

Read

A woman once entered her pastor's study and announced that she was angry at God. Her pastor asked her to explain. She shared with him the fact that she had been praying for months that the Lord would send someone into her life who could look after her elderly mother who was living in a faraway state. "I've asked Him over and over again for help and He seems to be turning a deaf ear to me," she said. "I'm so disappointed with God that I'm just about ready to tell Him that I don't think I need to pray. I think I'm just gonna jump on a plane and go take care of mother myself." Silence followed her statement. After a few reflective moments the woman looked at the pastor and said, "I think I just learned that I am God's answer to my prayer. I think He wants me to go and take care of my mother myself." She was right. God used her as an answer to her own prayers.

The same principle applies to the question of providing for our families. Jesus instructs us to pray, "Give us this day our daily bread," but He doesn't hereby want us to become idle, waiting for Him to place food in our mouths as if we were shrieking baby birds. Instead He desires us to use the skills, strength, and ability He has given us.

St. Paul supported himself as he planted churches. He writes to the Thessalonians, "We worked night and day, laboring and toiling so that we would not be a burden to any of you" (2 Thessalonians 3:8). Paul was able to work and so he did. He supported himself by making tents. By supporting himself he also gave no opportunity for people to suggest that he cost them more than he was worth.

Idleness is common in our present age. Much discussion has been offered over the appropriateness of welfare. A common argument against welfare is that it costs the taxpayers too much money. That may be true, but the godly man works and believes others should work, not because of the cost of idleness born by those who do work, but rather because of their need to work in order to give thanks and glory to God. In Colossians 3:23 Paul writes, "Whatever you do, work at it with all your heart, as working for the Lord, not for men." Through their work people worship and praise God. It is a healthy and wholesome activity. Through our work, we don't just participate with God in providing for our families, we also provide the world with an example of excellence. People who work heartily as serving the Lord and not men stand out like lights shining in the darkness. Our work provides people with an opportunity to see the difference Jesus makes in our lives.

REACT

1. Share with your group a time when you found that you were God's answer to your own prayer. How does that make you feel? How does this affect your confidence in the power of prayer?

2. The whole notion of providing for ourselves and our families is designed to make sure that we don't become a burden to anyone. Can you think of a set of circumstances where a man would have no choice but to be a burden to others? How might we assure this man of his worth?

3. How then can we work joyfully for employers who do not fully appreciate us?

4. If work is an act of worship, then what kind of worshiper are you: regular, enthusiastic, sporadic, or Christmas and Easter? What kind of worker does God desire us to be? Why?

Pride and Providing

Read

A man once found himself in tremendous financial difficulty. He owned his own business, but the business was doing poorly. This man urged his friends to pray that the Lord would bless his business so that he could provide for his family and the church. Each friend obliged. Despite the prayers his business did not improve. The man was plunged into a crisis of faith over the fact that God didn't seem to be hearing his cry for help. "Why does God keep me from growing my business?" he would ask. Finally one of his friends suggested that he give up the business and go to work for someone else. The man was offended by his friend's suggestion. He told his friend he would never work for anyone else because he could make more money working for himself. His friend responded, "It seems to me that a little money is better than no money."

This man could have provided comfortably for his family and his church if he would have sought employment. His pride wouldn't allow him to do so. His family paid a tremendous price in fear and uncertainty so that he could own his own business.

Men who know that they cannot accomplish anything in and of themselves also know that all things are possible

through Christ. The well-being of their families and their
need to offer their gifts and skills to God through honest work
are more important than their pride.

REACT

1. How can pride get in the way of a man's ability to provide for his family?

2. Read Proverb 16:18. Share stories or experiences
you've had that prove this passage is true.

3. What is the difference between having pride in your
work and being proud?

MAN of the YEAR

READ

In order to encourage men to strive for excellence in their
faith and the use of their God-given skills, a Lutheran congregation decided to give an annual award—"Man of the Year."

The congregation had a very difficult choice to make. God
had blessed them with many prominent men. Business own-
ers, physicians, lawyers, authors, educators, and athletes regularly occupied the pews. When the choice for "Man of the
Year" was made, the entire congregation was shocked.
Instead of choosing a man who was well educated and highly
thought of in the community, the congregation chose its own
custodian, also a member of the church. Jack, as he was
called, worked tirelessly for the church. He never complained

about the simpleness of his job, instead he tried to constantly outdo himself in maintaining the facility and serving the needs of the members. Jack treated every member of the church, even those who criticized him, with love and respect. "Sir" and "Ma'am" seemed to be his two favorite words. Jack's wife and children always attended church. People felt comfortable around Jack's children, often commenting on how respectful they were. Jack's family didn't have many things. One Sunday morning after a snowstorm the pastor arrived at church early to see that Jack had been there most of the night shoveling snow, making sure that the congregation would be able to enter the sanctuary and classroom buildings. Moved by his faithfulness, the pastor said, "Jack, you work way too hard for us." "Not as hard as Jesus worked for me," Jack replied.

When he presented the "Man of the Year" award to Jack, the congregational president said that Jack took pride in his work, pride in his church, pride in his God, pride in his family, and pride in himself. He provided the congregation with someone they could be proud of.

REACT

1. In light of Jack's story, is pride always wrong? When is pride a good thing?

2. What sorts of things can a man of God be proud of? Why?

3. What kinds of things does a faithful man like Jack provide for his family and friends?

What Else Should a Christian Man Provide for His Family?

Read

By the grace of God, Chris lived to the ripe old age of 92. He had raised his family during the depression and was grateful, all his life, for every blessing he received from the Lord.

While he was a wonderful worker, it was obvious to all that the most important things in Chris' life were his Lord and his family. Having successfully raised his children, he spent his retirement traveling all over the country in order to attend the baptisms, confirmations, graduations, and weddings of his grandchildren and great-grandchildren. They in turn traveled from all over the country to attend his funeral.

When the funeral was over, the family returned to Chris' house for food and fellowship. After most of the friends who came to pay their respects had eaten, fellowshiped, and left, the family gathered in a circle out in the afternoon sun and began to talk about Chris. For hours his wife, children, grandchildren, and great-grandchildren shared remembrances of Chris that all began with the phrase "What Grandpa gave to me was ..." The list of things that Chris gave his family included love, a sense of security, examples of forgiveness, a sense of importance, an understanding ear when no one else understood, a wonderful laugh, a strong faith in Jesus, a sense of what is important and what isn't, and an appreciation of family.

They talked for hours and not once did someone say that Chris had provided them with material possessions. Chris had been a good and careful provider but he would not be remembered as a provider of food, clothing, and shelter. Instead, he would be remembered as a man who provided his family with love, sincerity, honesty, humor, and hope. Despite his humble lifestyle, Chris had provided his family with everything they needed.

React

1. Take a moment and put your feet in Chris' shoes. Your own family has gathered together on the afternoon of your

funeral to share what you gave. What do you want them to remember you gave them?

2. Once you have listed the things you hope to provide your family, note next to each what you will do in order to provide these things.

Respond

In response to what God has done for you through Jesus Christ, plan to apply the principle of this chapter to your life by doing the following:

1. Remember that no matter how hard you work, God is the provider of all things.

2. Be grateful for the job you have and make it your business to work each day as though you were working for the Lord Himself.

3. Pray that the Lord enables you to demonstrate pride in Him as your provider and Savior.

4. Pray that the Lord empowers you to provide your family with a faithful witness to the love of God in Christ Jesus.

6

JESUS AS SON

Ready

Jesus had been up all night. During the night He had suffered the insult of neglect at the hands of His three closest disciples who slept instead of watching and praying with Him during His hour of need. Armed soldiers arrested Him. The Sanhedrin met illegally to decide His fate. He conversed with two prominent government officials. Neither wanted anything to do with Him. In order to placate an irritated crowd, Pilate had Jesus receive 39 lashes with leather strips that had pieces of metal and the ankle bones of sheep attached to them. Once His flesh had been ripped, soldiers further destroyed His dignity by placing a crown of thorns on His head, a purple robe on His shoulders, and a reed in His hand. He was placed on display before the angry crowd. Pilate hoped that the crowd's hostility would subside once they saw the pain and shame to which Jesus had been subjected. It didn't work. They shouted, "Crucify Him! Crucify Him!" Pilate turned Jesus over to them. Jesus felt the weight of His cross placed upon His shoulders. In His already seriously weakened condition, He carried the cross to Golgotha, the place of death. Once at Golgotha the soldiers stripped Him. His clothes were divided and the flesh of His hands and feet were ripped as He was nailed to a cross.

He fought for every breath as He hung from the cross. The cursing and swearing of his co-crucified filled His ears along with the taunting of the people who surrounded the cross.

A lesser man would have returned the slurs. Most crucified men spent their last hours on earth cursing those who executed them. But not Jesus. Despite the pain, Jesus focused on His responsibilities. He focused on the responsibility of being the "Lamb of God who takes away the sin of the world."

And He focused on His responsibility to "honor His Father and mother."

Any other man would have been blinded by the pain and injustice. Jesus looked down from the cross and saw His mother. Perhaps He recalled the stories she told Him about the visit of the angel who had informed her that she was to be the mother of the Savior of the world. Perhaps He remembered the stories of the star, and the Wise Men, the shepherds, and His family's flight into Egypt. Undoubtedly, He remembered that His mother had loved Him. With all the love His broken body could muster, He summoned His mother and His dear friend John to the cross and said, "Woman, here is your son," and to the disciple, "Here is your mother." With this gracious act Jesus had once again fulfilled all that the law required of Him.

Honoring God's Gifts to Us

Read

Martin Luther was once asked why he loved his wife Katie. His answer was simple, humorous, and profound. He said, "Because she is God's gift to me, and other women have greater faults." Luther's words also speak to those of us who are sons. We are called by God to honor our parents if for no other reason than they are God's gift to us.

The Third Commandment doesn't call us to obey, understand, or adore our parents. It simply tells us to honor them. God knows that every parent is sinful. Sinful parents sometimes ask their children to do things that are not God pleasing. God would not expect us to obey them at those times. But even though their sins may disappoint, we are still told to honor our parents. We may think that some of the habits, practices, and beliefs of our parents are absolutely foolish, maybe even comical. Still, we honor God when we honor them.

Once again Jesus doesn't ask us to do something He hasn't already done. Jesus honored His earthly father and mother and in so doing also honored His Father in heaven. We know that Jesus honored His Father by being about His Father's business. Jesus committed Himself to accomplish the goals and purposes of His Father. From His youth Jesus was in the temple or synagogue on the Sabbath and on feast days. Jesus was a man of prayer. He spent time communicating with His Father in heaven. When tempted by the devil in the wilderness, Jesus refused to disrespect His Father and give allegiance to the devil. When Jesus saw that others disrespected His Father and His Father's Word, Jesus supported His Father without regard to His own reputation. Ultimately, Jesus honored His Father when He was arrested, tried, and crucified. Although He was well aware of the pain His Father's mission would bring to Him, He remained obedient.

REACT

Recall Jesus' relationship with His parents, earthly and heavenly, as you respond to the following situations.

1. Your parents ask if they could visit you and your family on Sunday afternoon. You inform them that you have an afternoon commitment at church and ask them to come on Sunday evening. Your statement and request hurts your parents' feelings. They can't understand how you would choose church over your parents. They finish their conversation by saying, "Thank you for showing us where we fit into your life!" How might you respond to your parents in such a way as to honor them?

2. Your nephew needs a job. Your nephew has a reputation of being irresponsible and has proven that he has trouble holding a job. At the tender age of 17, he's already lost two jobs. Your mother has asked you for months to see if there is an opening for him in your company. You have shared your concerns with her and tell her that when you think your nephew is responsible enough to keep a job, you will consider offering him one. At Christmas dinner your mother announces to everyone at the table, including your nephew,

that you intend to give him a job. How can you respond to this situation in such a way as to continue to honor your mother?

3. You've learned that you have terminal cancer. Your physicians inform you that you will need to undergo surgery, radiation, and chemotherapy. The prognosis is not good. When you tell your mother what you have learned, the first words out of her mouth are, "What will happen to me now?" How will you respond?

4. God has been good to you. He has seen you through good times and bad times. He has blessed your family with good health and love. You take comfort daily from the fact that no matter what happens to you or your family members, you will spend eternity together in heaven. What can you as God's son do to honor your heavenly Father?

Reflect

1. Honoring implies that a son will acknowledge the rightful place of his parents in his life. Persons who honor their parents have contact with them: they talk, they make plans together, they enjoy each other's company. What would Jesus say about the son who fails to acknowledge the presence of his parents in his life?

2. Honoring means to lift someone up. Our natural human spirit—sinful and unclean—drives us to tear people down instead of lifting them up. Think of ways that Jesus' power can enable you to lift your parents up in honor.

How Do You Honor Your Parents?

Read

When a son is three years old, he looks at his father and thinks to himself, "This is the biggest, kindest person I know." When the child is 10 years old, he looks at his father and says, "My dad is bigger, stronger, and smarter than anyone else's dad. He could 'beat up' every other father in the world." When the child is 16, he looks at his father and says, "How could anyone know so little? The world has passed my dad by." When the child is 21, he looks at his father and says, "Dad's done a few things well in his life, maybe I could ask him what he thinks about my problems." At age 30 the son looks at his father and says, "I really like to hear him talk. Dad has a lot of wisdom. I could do worse than follow the example of how he lived his life." At age 40 the child remembers his father and says, "Dad had such wisdom, I sure wish he was here to help me now." At age 50 the child remembers his father and says, "He was the wisest man I ever knew, I hope I can just accomplish half of what he accomplished."

This little story indicates that often children fail to honor their parents. The self-centered teenager sees his parents as residents of the "olden days" completely incapable of living in the "real world." The older, wiser, child who has begun to face life's challenges begins to appreciate the way his parents handled problems. Suddenly, Mom and Dad have become very bright. When his parents are gone, the child realizes that his parents were not obstacles to his development but instead teachers, coaches, and mentors. He remembers his parents and wishes they were still there to give him the benefit of their knowledge. We might say, "Immature people have trouble honoring their parent. People who are mature in Christ love to honor their parents."

Children who honor their parents know God gave parents as a gift to them. Children who honor their parents also demonstrate maturity in knowing that their parents are not perfect, just as they are not perfect. They remember the times they disappointed their parents. They remember the times they told their parents a lie. They understand that people who are by nature "sinful and unclean" will always at times disappoint others. So instead of being undone because of their parents' disappointing behavior, they speak to them the forgiveness of sins, they look upon their parents just as Christ looks upon them—"sinners" and "saints" to whom Jesus has entrusted the maintenance and growth of His kingdom.

Growing old is mandatory, growing up is optional. The grown-up child is the child who honors his parents. Jesus never tires of helping us grow up in the faith. Like a loving father, whenever we fail in relationship with our parents, Jesus is there to pick us up, forgive us, and send us out to serve again, refreshed by His love.

Mature Christian men honor their parents by ...

1. Understanding that they are worth something. Not everyone's parent is capable of being a great volunteer, worker, or grandparent. Some parents are physically impaired and so do little that seems to be constructive day in and day out. Other parents seem to be overcome with a negative spirit that expresses itself in constant criticism that doesn't build up, but tears down. Regardless of our parents' mental, physical, or spiritual condition, the mere fact that they are still alive means that God is not finished with them yet. We can honor our parents by treating them as people who are capable of making a contribution to our lives. We can invite them to our homes. We can seek their advise on certain issues. We can speak well of them in public. We can tell them that we are glad that God made them our parents.

2. Listening to them. Good listeners make good students, good friends, good employees, good spouses, and good sons. There is no greater way for one person to honor another person than to listen to her/him. Listening doesn't imply that you do everything your parents tell you. It simply means to hear what they are saying and respond in such a way as to let them know that you respect their words and their wisdom. Certainly parents who care about their children's lives will be quick to give advice when the children face a change or a challenge. Sometimes the advice is helpful, sometimes not. We don't owe our parents the honor of doing everything they ask us to do. But we do owe them the honor of letting them know that we appreciate the concern expressed in their words.

When we don't feel like listening to our parents, Jesus who lives in our hearts through faith enables us to open our ears toward those we love. Certainly there will be times that we fail. Then Jesus forgives us for our impatience or selfishness and strengthens us to care for our parents, regardless of the inconvenience.

3. Remembering the significant days in their lives. An older gentleman became depressed at every major holiday. His family detected his depression and of course inquired as to its source. The man would always reassure them that there was nothing wrong. His children didn't believe him and

talked about their concern for their father every chance they got. Sometimes these conversations took place in the presence of their young children. The following Christmas one of his grandchildren, a 10-year-old boy, sat next to him and said, "Grandpa, why do you get sad every Christmas?" The man took a deep breath. He realized that there was no hiding his depression. He didn't wish to worry his grandchild. So he shared the fact that all of his relatives who shared most of his life were dead. It made him sad to think about Christmases past and that no one in the world had the same memories he had.

When a son remembers the birthday, anniversary, or other significant date in the life of his parents, he lets them know that he is paying attention and that he cares. Our parents know how busy we are. They know how easy it would be to forget them. Remembering these days let's them know that they are as precious to you as they are to God.

4. Not arguing with them. When our parents question our motives or our actions, it's easy to argue with them. But those men who know that their parents are God's gift to them choose to deal with them in love. Jesus who loves and forgives us enables us to respect our parents by not arguing. Arguing may enable us to feel that we are being strong. This may be a victory in the world, but in the kingdom of God it is a loss. In Christ's kingdom the victory is won when people approach the criticism of their parents with the words of St. Paul ringing in their ears, "Do not think of yourself more highly than you ought" and "but in humility consider others better than yourselves." When we embrace the message of these verses, Jesus enables His love to shine through our hearts as we build up our parents and in so doing His kingdom.

REACT

What behaviors can men practice that tell their parents of their worth?

Have This Attitude among Yourselves

Read

Being a God-pleasing son to our parents is a matter of attitude. Careful reflection on anyone's relationship with their parents would reveal failures. There are times when we are wrapped up in ourselves. We can't see how anything could be the "right way" unless it is "our way." People who live like this in relation to their parents are doomed to heartbreak. This heartbreak is not necessary because we are the sons of a God who daily gives us a new heart and a new mind through faith in Christ Jesus. That new heart and mind give us a new attitude, the attitude of Jesus. "Your attitude should be the same as that of Christ Jesus: Who, being in very nature God, did not consider equality with God something to be grasped, but made Himself nothing, taking the very nature of a servant, being made in human likeness. And being found in appearance as a man, He humbled Himself and became obedient to death—even death on a cross!" (Philippians 2:6–8).

This attitude is God's gift to us in Christ. When exercised, it results in families in which people are respected and everyone's need for love is met. If things have gone well between you and your parents, rejoice. If they haven't, don't give up hope. It's never too late for Jesus' love to change things. God can and does perform miracles in the hearts of people. This miracle began when the Holy Spirit working through the Gospel placed saving faith in your heart—the moment when God through His Son's death on the cross claimed you who was once His enemy—as a son, an heir of heaven.

A middle-aged pastor once told his vicar the story of his ordination. It was a great day he said. The congregation he would serve came out in large numbers. The choir had rehearsed several beautiful pieces. He was honored that a large number of pastors came to participate in the ordination even though they had to travel many miles. The sermon was memorable. The pastor said he would never forget what happened to him after his fellow pastors placed their hands upon him to bless him. He remembered hearing a small commotion going on in the pews right behind him. He saw the pastor who stood before him as he knelt, focusing his attention on someone who was coming forward. It was the new pastor's father. His father announced, "If there is no objection, I would also like to bless my son." Having said that he placed his hands on his son's head and said. "Lord, this is Jimmy, my son, make him a good pastor to these people, and while he may be their pastor, tonight I thank You that he is my son, my son in whom I am well pleased. Thanks for giving him to me. Amen."

What more could any son ask than that his own children would say the same thing about him. May God grant this to us all.

Respond

1. Plan to give your parent(s) a gift. It could something simple such as flowers, or a cake, or pictures of your family. Make sure to give it to them on a day other than an anniversary or birthday. Just let them know that you think about them often.

2. The next time you visit your parents promise yourself that you will work hard to listen to them first and then act. Pay close attention to how well you do. Was it easy? difficult? Did you feel as though you were blessing your parents, or did you feel that you were letting your parents take advantage of the conversation? Why?

3. Sit with your parents and thank them for raising you. Share with them some remembrances of your childhood. Try to end the conversation with a phrase something like: "I just want you to know how fortunate it is that God chose me to be your son." Think about additional ways you can affirm your parents.

Answers and Comments

Man as Teacher

Opening

Pray together that the Lord would show you those opportunities you have to serve a teacher.

Ready

Read aloud the introductory paragraphs. Have the men take a few minutes to think about men who have served as good teachers in their lives. None of these men have to be trained teachers; fellow workers, family members, and friends will do. Characteristics will vary.

Teaching by Example
Read

Read the story of the angry man. For fun you might want one man to read the part of the pastor and another man the part of the angry man.

React

Discuss the questions.

1. Don't be surprised if most of the men believe the man's response is normal and usual.

2. Jimmy's dad was a teacher. He may or may not have taught intentionally. In an attempt to teach Jimmy to take care of himself, Jimmy's dad also taught Jimmy that fighting was acceptable behavior.

3. Don't be surprised if most men find this response typical.

4. The pastor taught them that might does not make right in the kingdom of God. In this kingdom grace and mercy are key.

5. The explanation here is more important than the answer. When we begin to understand the motives behind our actions, we can begin to grow.

6. Through the pastor's message of God's love and forgiveness through Jesus, the Holy Spirit will work to heal relationships broken by sin.

The Man Who Teaches for God Models Love

Read

Have the men read the Bible passages and note the specific things that God teaches in each of the passages.

React

1. We show our love for God as we love our neighbors. Our neighbor is every other person.

2. Love those who persecute you. God's love for us in Jesus "while we were still sinners" motivates us to love others.

3. Christians demonstrate their discipleship by their love for others. As Jesus first loved us, we love others.

4. The foundation of good works is God's love for us in Christ Jesus. By God's grace alone through faith alone in the person and work of Jesus Christ we are set free from sin, death, and the power of the devil. God equips us through faith to serve Him with good works.

Love Is a Verb Not Only a Noun

Read

Have the men read this passage from Matthew 18. Help them see that those who are forgiven are also forgiving.

React

1. Jesus taught forgiveness by His words and His actions, particularly His action on our behalf on the cross. Without the forgiveness of sins Jesus earned for us on the cross, all people would be lost forever. Our greatest witness to Jesus is the forgiveness we share.

2. Most would consider the king's actions foolish.

3. The king probably expected the servant to be humble and grateful.

4. We respond to the riches of forgiveness we have received by failing at times to forgive others. We are quicker to judge than to forgive.

5. His own forgiveness had taught him nothing. He possibly believed the king had given him what he deserved.

6. We teach Jesus' forgiveness by our words and actions of love and forgiveness.

Teaching through Failing

Read

Read aloud the story.

React

1. Brainstorm ways Joe could handle this problem. Answers will vary.

2. Answers will vary.

Read

Read aloud the ending to the story of Joe.

React

1. Answers will vary. Jesus' love and forgiveness empower us to confess our sins to others we have hurt and to forgive those who have hurt us.

2. As those who have been redeemed by Christ the Crucified, we can view mistakes as opportunities to grow through forgiveness—the forgiveness of God in Christ and the forgiveness we share with others.

The Center of Jesus' Teaching

Read

Help the men to understand that the Law accuses and gives death, while the Gospel forgives and gives life.

React

1. Answers will vary. Point out that only *d* is scriptural. The others all include errors.

2. We teach by example and words. Share the importance of telling others of the reason for the forgiveness you request and share—Jesus Christ crucified.

3. Comfort, security, cooperation, and love grow.

Respond

1. God Himself in His Word commands me to teach my

family the truth of His great love and forgiveness through faith in Christ Jesus.

2. This will take time, but it's worth it. Remember for your failures Jesus offers His forgiveness.

3. Again, encourage the men to follow through on this activity.

4. Have the men share their responses with each other.

Man as Spiritual Leader

Open

Open with a prayer that asks God to show us the spiritual gifts He has given to us and to others and to empower us to help others receive Jesus as Lord and Savior and serve Him with all our gifts.

Leaders and Their Leadership Style
Ready

Help the men compare the leadership style of Jesus, including recruitment and inspiration, with the leadership style of other leaders.

Stories of Leadership
Read/React

Matthew 3:13–17—Jesus fulfilled all that the Law required of us. Jesus "walked the walk" expected of all those who follow Him.

Matthew 6:1–18—Jesus teaches humility. Jesus teaches us how to pray as He prays. Again, Jesus not only tells but does.

Matthew 7:1–5—Jesus tells us not to judge others. His death on the cross won forgiveness for all sins.

Matthew 9:10–13—Jesus accepts all people, even the most despised sinners.

Respond

Encourage the men to make this a sincere reflection of what Jesus thinks they need and not what they think they need. Remind the participants that Jesus not only "talked the talk" but also "walked the walk." He was quick to forgive, to accept, and to love.

Spiritual Gifts and Spirit-led Leaders
Read

Read carefully the information regarding the gifts of the Holy Spirit. Emphasize that each baptized child of God has received some of these gifts, but not everyone has received the same gifts. When you get to the explanation of the gifts, have each man read a few as you go around the room.

React

1. Absolutely nothing. All spiritual gifts are undeserved gifts from God.
2. Answers will vary.
3. Encourage participants to brainstorm together how specific gifts could be used in service to Christ's church.

Leading God's Gifted
Read

Have the men read about Paul's leadership to the congregations. Then read the story of the pastor and the little girl, Dorothy.

React

1. Answers will vary.
2. A true leader not only "talks the talk," but also "walks the walk." The most effective leaders lead not only by their words but also by their example.
3. This may be hard for some. Avoid criticizing others as the answers are shared.
4. Hopefully answers will include words such as sincerity, selflessness, faithfulness, and humility. Boasting, arrogance, pride, and sectarianism will not lead people to know the servant Jesus who in His greatest act of leadership willingly went to the cross to suffer and die for the sins of all people.
5. Answers will vary.

Sprit-led Leaders Are Honest
Read

Read and discuss the material.

Spirit-led Leaders Are Humble

Read aloud this section. Discuss how Christian leaders serve for Jesus' sake and reputation, not their own sake and reputation.

Respond

1. Challenge the men to go through this exercise and bring their results back next week. Compare and contrast their findings.
2. Encourage the men to begin or continue family devotions.
3. Encourage the men to worship faithfully. Remind them that we lead most effectively as we not only "talk the talk" but also "walk the walk."

Man as Lover

Opening

Pray that the Lord would help us through the study of His Word learn to love the world by laying down our lives for others just as He did.

Ready

Have the men read this section and think about how Jesus is the true "lover."

Love Given, Lost, and Restored
Read

Read aloud the story of creation and the fall. Help the men to understand how sin has distorted and destroyed God's original concept of love and how through Christ He restored love to a sinful world. Jesus the "lover" of all souls enables and empowers us to be lover to all people.

React

1. Attitudes that focus on negative characteristics can destroy a relationship. In spite of the ugliness of our sin Jesus suffered and died for us. His love alone empowers us to look beyond faults and love as He first loved us.

2. It is sinful to take advantage of or make fun of another human being. Such talk turns a precious child of God into a thing. Although sin might cause us to justify this behavior as normal, it is not—it is sin. Jesus' love for us empowers us to affirm the worth of all people.

3. It hurts to be treated as a "thing." Generally there is little we can do to change the mind and heart of a person who enjoys using people. But all things are possible through Christ. As we love those who persecute us, they may question where the ability to love comes from.

4. Sexual harassment would be a thing of the past.

Laying Down Your Life for Your Friends
Read

Read and discuss each of the situations considering how we as "lovers" would react to others.

React

1. Listen to the responses to the question. Pay particular attention to the difference that may appear between the way the father and the pastor deal with Donald.

2. Again, listen to the responses to the question. Pay close attention to the difference that may appear between the way the father and the pastor deal with Deborah.

3. Pay close attention to a standard that says men can participate in sexual sin without receiving the same judgment as women.

4. Again listen carefully for any double standard.

5. Jesus might ask Deborah and Donald whom they have served as they were sexually intimate. Sexual love outside of marriage is self-serving. Within the one flesh union of marriage, God enables a couple to serve each other as they exercise their intimate expression of sexuality. No doubt Deborah and Donald need to hear God's Law. And as they confess their sinful, self-centered behaviors, they need to hear the Gospel.

Love and Marriage
Read

Read aloud the explanation of Ephesians 5:22.

React

1. Taken out of context, Ephesians 5:22 sets the stage for abuse, considering a wife as property, and dissension.

2. Ephesians 5:22 is often used out of context to describe the way a woman is to relate to her husband. However Ephesians 5:21 and 23 are key verses that lead to proper understanding of verse 22 and to a healthy relationship between a husband and wife. God desires all those who have received His love and forgiveness in faith to submit to one another.

3. Empowered by Jesus' love, the husband will relate to and care for his wife humbly and selflessly.

Laying Down Your Life

Read/React

1. *a* and *b* are typical responses. *c* is a response that flows from the mouth of one who has experienced the magnitude of Jesus' love.

2. *b* and *e*   4. *d*
3. *d*   5. *d*

Confess together the fact that at times your response to situations such as these may be less than God desires. At those moments the Lover of your soul, Jesus, invites you to confess your sins and receive the love and forgiveness He earned for you through His death on the cross. Renewed by His love He empowers you to be a lover of souls by your action and in your words.

Respond

Each of the four suggested activities requires a thoughtful response.

Man as Father

Opening

In the opening prayer ask the Lord to place His own Fatherly heart into yours as you study His Word.

Abba! Father!

Ready

As you read the introductory section, pay close attention to those things that separate a father from a good dad.

Biblical CHARActERistics of DAds
Read

Read aloud and discuss this section.

React

1. Answers may vary.
2. A father who depends upon his heavenly Father to guide and to sustain him will make decisions trusting confidently in the wisdom only God can provide. As the Holy Spirit strengthens faith through God's Word, the father makes decisions for his children in and for their interest.
3. Through worship and Bible study the Holy Spirit works to strengthen saving faith in the crucified and risen Savior. When we neglect the means of God's grace, we cut ourselves off from that which strengthens our relationship with God and others.
4. Listening enables us to care for our children's needs and not just our own.
5. A father who confesses his sins and asks for forgiveness models the relationship that exists between God and him to his children. Confession indicates a desire to take responsibility for one's actions and to build stronger relationships.

DAd thE MERciful
Read

As you read this section, emphasize all the examples of mercy apparent in the scriptural references.

React

1. It would be simple if knowledge of right and wrong was the only challenge. We do well to remember that children are sinful human beings who sometimes know the right but choose to do the wrong.
2. That's fine as long as we remember the place where Jesus would put the child.
3. Children need to experience consequences for their sinful behavior. As they repent, they need to experience the embrace of love and mercy.
4. We need to bear our children's burdens with them to demonstrate our concern and love.
5. Responsibility is necessary. Grace enables people to grow.

Adoption

Read

Notice carefully how the practice of adopting a child in Rome parallels the way God adopted us in Christ.

React

1. Each and every day given by God is a new day. Our old sins are not held against us, instead God in Christ has forgiven and forgotten them.

2. Answers will vary. As we speak words of love to them and act in love to them, we demonstrate that they are wanted.

Call Me Daddy, Please!

Read

After they have read the story, ask the men how they feel about being called "daddy."

React

1. Children who use the word *daddy* to refer to their fathers indicate their love and affection. Men who are called "daddy" have earned the love and respect of their children.

2. Take time to do this exercise. Answers will vary.

Dads Leave an Inheritance for Their Children

Read

Explain to the men that some inheritances, especially a spiritual inheritance, are greater than any material inheritance.

React

1. The spiritual inheritance is the only inheritance your children can take with them into eternity.

2. Lovingly share with your children how the inheritance of faith is the greatest gift they could ever receive.

Respond

1. Scripture bears the truth of this message.

2. Our heavenly Father can serve as a wonderful model for dads.

3. He shares His word of forgiveness and love.

Man as Provider

Leadership Style and Purpose
Ready

Compare the difference between the way men would provide for their families and the way God would have us provide for our families. Pay close attention to the focus of the trust.

Leading toward Peace
Read

Read aloud this section.

React

1. Extremely difficult because our sin forces us to think that we and we alone are responsible for our well-being.

2. God is eager to help. His help is not conditional on our ability to help ourselves.

3. We seek first His kingdom as we rely upon Him for all of our needs, including our greatest need—forgiveness of sins and eternal life through His Son's death on the cross.

Enough Is Enough
Read

Read aloud this section or invite volunteers to read it aloud.

React

1. Answers will vary. By world standards many would not consider this success.

2. God measures success not by what we can accumulate and store but what we give. The greatest success that we could enjoy would be to give to our families the gift of faith in Jesus that God has first given us.

Is Money the Root of All Evil?
Read

Help the men to recognize that money is not the root of all evil, the *love* of money is. The love of money gets in the way of our love for God.

React

Yes. True greatness comes only from that which God provides through faith in Jesus—forgiveness of sins and eternal life.

WE HAVE MORE THINGS TO SUPPORT THAN OUR FAMILIES

Read

Help the men see that God intends for them to provide for their families. He also intends for them to provide for His church.

React

1. The people of God whom He has blessed richly desire to share His blessings with the church, so that through its work many will come to know Jesus as Lord and Savior.

2. We can support the ministry of our church by offering our time and talents. Have participants brainstorm specific ways they can share their time and talents.

IF GOD IS OUR PROVIDER, WHERE DO WE FIT IN?

Read

As the men read this story, help them understand that sometimes they are God's answer to their prayers.

React

1. Answers will vary.

2. Accidents or poor health could disable a man from working. To the person who is unable to work, we can share our love and support as we remind him of the worth Jesus won for him on the cross.

3. We who have received salvation in Christ are motivated to work at our jobs as though we were working for the Lord.

4. Answers will vary. God desires that we work joyfully in service to Him.

PRIDE AND PROVIDING

Read

Pride can get in the way of our providing for our families. Through Christ we can put aside our sinful pride to do that which is best for ourselves and our families.

React

1. Pride can keep a man from doing that which is best for himself and his family.

2. Discuss the proverb in a free and nonjudgmental way.

3. A man who is proud of his work knows that God has equipped him for his work.

Man of the Year

Read

In the kingdom of God the "Man of the Year" reflects God's love in humility, hard work, and love.

React

1. Pride is not wrong when it is pride in serving the one who served us first—Jesus Christ.

2. A man can be proud of his God and the opportunities God provides him to use the gifts God has given him.

3. Jack provided love that flowed from the love of God in Christ Jesus.

What Else Should a Christian Man Provide for His Family?

Read

Read aloud the story of Chris.

React

1. Answers will vary.
2. Answers will vary.

Respond

Urge the men to complete the suggested activity.

Man as Son

Jesus as Son

Ready

Help the men see the pain that Jesus endured. In spite of His suffering He continued to care for His mother.

Honoring God's Gifts to Us

Read

Help the participants recognize that men of Christ are empowered by His love to honor their parents.

React

1. Answers will vary. Tell them how much they mean to you, but you cannot break a previous commitment.

2. Answers will vary. Speak to your mother in private, sharing the uncomfortable position in which she has put you. Then share your concerns in private with your nephew.

3. Answers will vary. In private speak the truth in love. At times it may be difficult, if not impossible, to honor our parents. Only God's love in Christ enables us to put other's concerns above our own concerns.

4. We honor God as we serve, praise, and thank Him for His love.

Reflect

1. The son who fails to acknowledge his parents misses a tremendous blessing.

2. Answers will vary.

How Do You Honor Your Parents?

Read

Help the men see that the ability to honor is directly tied to personal maturity.

React

Listening to our parents and affirming them demonstrates their worth to us. By remembering their birthdays, anniversaries, and other significant days in their lives we demonstrate to them how important they are to us.

Have This Attitude among Yourselves

Read

Help the men to understand that the attitude of Christ is a gift received through faith that can bring peace and happiness to a family.

Respond

Urge participants to complete the suggested activities.